Uncle Mickey the Barber
and Other Stories

by

Dr. Douglas Lobay, N.D.

D1738158

A collection of stories and defining moments of
my childhood and youth growing up in the
Sunshine Valley in southern British Columbia.

Published by
Dr. Douglas Lobay, ND
Kelowna, BC

Disclaimer: The information presented here in this book is for educational and entertainment purposes only and is not intended as a substitute for the diagnosis and/or treatment of disease. Individuals should seek out proper medical care from licensed health care professional for appropriate diagnosis and treatment.

Canadian Cataloguing Publication Data
Lobay, Doug, 1965 –

ISBN: 978-09695681-4-8
Non-fiction, 1. Autobiography, 2. History, 3. Humour

Table of Contents

Dedication

To my children Rachel and Jessica for their endless love and
support. Thanks for the countless hours of watching the Big Bang
Theory, Friends and How I Met Your Mother.

Acknowledgements

I would like to thank:
My Mom and Dad
Arlene, Jim and Bobby
Mike and Annette
Mike and Nellie
Susan Carroll
Dr. Ursula Harlos
Dr. Janice Potter
Rachel and Jessica
And of course, Natalie

Preface

When asked "How would you have lived your life differently if you had a chance?" Nadine Stair, an 85-year-old woman, from Louisville, Kentucky, provided these poetic words as her response.

"If I had my life to live over again, I'd dare to make more mistakes next time. I'd relax. I'd limber up. I'd be sillier than I've been this trip. I would take fewer things seriously. I would take more chances, I would eat more ice cream and less beans. I would, perhaps, have more actual troubles but fewer imaginary ones. You see, I'm one of those people who was sensible and sane, hour after hour, day after day. Oh, I've had my moments. If I had to do it over again, I'd have more of them. In fact, I'd try to have nothing else- just moments, one after another, instead of living so many years ahead of each day. I've been one of those persons who never goes anywhere without a thermometer, a hot-water bottle, a raincoat, and a parachute. If I could do it again, I would travel lighter than I have. If I had to live my life over, I would start barefoot earlier in the spring and stay that way later in the fall. I would go to more dances, I would ride more merry-go-rounds, I would pick more daisies."

The 19th century author, essayist and Minister Ralph Waldo Emerson wrote these sage words about what it means to be successful in life.

"To laugh often and much; To win the respect of intelligent people and the affection of children; To earn the appreciation of honest critics and endure the betrayal of false friends; To appreciate beauty, to find the best in others; To leave the world a bit better, whether by a healthy child, a garden patch, or a redeemed social condition; To know even one life has breathed easier because you have lived. This is to have succeeded."

Introduction

This is the story of my life. This book is an anthology or collection of short stories about defining moments in my early childhood, youth and early adulthood. They are events that had some dramatic and profound effect of me. They were directing, influencing and life altering. They all had a positive or uplifting effect on me in some way. Some of these events were happy and some were sad. Most of the time there was a profound meaning, a nugget of truth or a pearl of wisdom. Looking back, I usually learnt something. These events and stories are all real and happened as best as I can remember.

Traditional autobiographies that list events and times in chronological order are usually boring and mundane. Life is a series of up and downs, punctuated by occurrences that are ground breaking and life altering. Very seldom does life proceed along in a linear fashion. It is a vast collections of experiences and incidents that occur in dramatic and often surprising fashion. These events almost occur in the fashion similar to the extinction of the dinosaurs. Things were going all fine till one day a mass extinction occurred. It was relatively fast, sudden and unexpected. It changed life in a rather exceptional and phenomenal manner. Such are the events and occurrences that shape a person's life. They are largely unexpected and nonetheless, life changing.

The first story I wrote was about my Uncle Mickey Ogloff. He was the town barber for many years and he lived on a small farm in the Nursery part of Grand Forks. He was a genuine character and fixture of life in a small town. He was born a Russian Doukhobor Christian, but he ate meat, drank alcohol and was a hunter and trapper. He was interesting fellow who believed in his own philosophy. He read a lot and was well informed just about everything. He taught me to believe in yourself and think for yourself.

Bobby and Me is a story about my older brother Bobby. He was my older sibling who took care of me and nurtured me. I talk about each member of my beloved family and the dynamic relationships we shared. I do a good characterization of my father George, my mother Marion, my older brother Jim, younger sister Arlene and of course, Bobby. The story culminates in the auto accident that claimed Bobby's life and its ultimate impact in our family afterwards.

George the Mechanic is a discussion about my father George. I start with his immigration Canada from Eastern Europe and then how his life developed and grew with his family. He was a strong and skilled mechanic who was the patriarch of our family. I discuss some of his personality traits and things that he did in life. I also talk about his hobbies and emphasize his love of nature and the outdoors. I close with a brief discussion of his shortcomings.

Hockey, Saddle Lake and the Big, Bad Bruins is the story about how hockey impacted my life. I skated and played hockey since I was four or five years old. I loved the game and it was an integral part of our family life. I played in our local minor hockey association from atoms to midgets. I played some junior B and in college and university. Some of best friends are people I have met through hockey. I still enjoy playing the game today.

Toil and Peaceful life is about a few relatives and family friends who shared a common ancestry and background. My mother was of a Russian Doukhobor background and my father was Polish, Russian and Ukrainian descent. Many of my friends also shared the same lineage. I talk about two aunts, Little Totya and Jane and how they influenced me. I then talk about an older farm couple who shared a bond of love even though they had trouble showing it. I also discuss how this old culture was integrated into a blended mosaic in Canada.

Volcanic Brown and the North Fork Valley describes my adventures and exploration in the wild valley to the north of Grand Forks. I first wrote an article for the local newspaper called the Grand Forks Gazette when I was a teenager. The story was on a miner named Volcanic Brown that lived up the North Fork at the turn of the 19th century. A mountain with a bright reddish brown patch is named after him at about 17 kilometres or 11 miles up the valley. Afterwards I talk about my exploits and escapades at different times and places around the valley.

Bill Barlee and Jolly Jack's Lost Gold Mine pays homage to N.L. Barlee for inspiring me about local history. When I was a teenager I used to read Mr. Barlee's books and magazine about the local history around Grand Forks and the Boundary Country. I used to drive around and search old ghost towns, forlorn mines and decrepit railways for relics of the past. I had gold pans and a sluice boxes that I used at various creeks around the region. Lost gold mines and buried treasures danced in my head. I also describe two inspiring and chance encounters with Mr. Barlee.

Phoenix and the Tamaracks discusses my times exploring the mountains around the old ghost of Phoenix located between Grand Forks and Greenwood. I rehash the old history of this infamous mining city from its glory to its demise. I then discuss my experiences in this area with activities such as alpine skiing, cross country skiing, getting firewood and hiking. I was particularly fond of the incredible natural beauty that was Phoenix and the colourful larch trees that adorned the landscape around there.

Faron, my Huckleberry Friend is a cute story of my relationship with my childhood friend who reminded me of Huckleberry Finn. He was a wild and free spirit who had a genuine love of girls, the outdoors and having fun. I recite some our fun times and misadventures from driving a tractor to being on the track and field together. I also talk about a sense of loss and the passage of time.

GFSS and Other Social Deviations delves into my times and experiences at Grand Forks Secondary School. Teenage adolescence is often a period of intense growth and development. It is also a time of awkwardness and learning where you belong in the world. I talk about my group of friends there and how I fit in there.

Fred W. and Mr. H. discusses the importance and lasting impact a good teacher can make on your life. A teacher is an indelible part of your life throughout your school career. I point out the values and characteristics of a good teacher. I then talk about how and why this teacher influenced me and made a positive lasting impact on my life. I further discuss another teacher who made an incredible impact my daughter's during her school experience.

Uncle Mickey the Barber

Loresa, Tamara and Michelle from Hardy Mountain describes my relationship to three girls that I met in school. From a first kiss, to an unfulfilled dream and unrequited love I bumble through the sometimes tricky and uncomfortable social awkwardness of dating and the opposite sex. I also elaborate on my special relationship of my old Honda 250 cc motorcycle and the freedom of the hills it afforded me.

The Gazette, the Highways and the Forestry is about my odd jobs and work experience in Grand Forks. My first real job was working as a janitor at the local newspaper called the Grand Forks Gazette. My second job was working as a rodman on a survey crew for the Ministry of Transportation and Highways. And my third job was working as a firefighter on an Initial Attack crew for the Ministry of Forestry. They were all fun jobs and I learned a lot from them and made a little money. I also had some interesting encounters and experiences with the people I worked with.

The Kettle River Raft Race is the story about my experience and misfortune at the Lions Club Raft Race. The raft race was held on the Father's Day weekend in the middle of June of each year on the Kettle River. It was a wild race with many entrants to see who could paddle the fastest down the river from Carson to City Park. At City Park there was a festive, carnival atmosphere with a big crowd, entertainment and fast food and drinks. My friend Faron and I went in the raft race and one the event one year.

Occam's Razor and Henry Thoreau describes the law of parsimony and how it relates to me and my life. It is a dictum of using simplicity in all parts of your life. I talk about growing up in a small town and reading books like Walden by Henry Thoreau. I then apply this axiom as it applies to more contemporary parts of life like diet and nutrition.

The Komodo Dragon Legend is a phantasmagoric story I told my children and their cousins about a stealth Komodo dragon living in the natural highlands just above our home. I weave the tale by taking my two daughters and their cousins in search of this mythical monster. The story centers around the older mischievous cousin Misha and his perception of this legend and relationship with my daughters

John Bastyr and UW is about my time spent in Seattle, Washington going to school at the Bastyr College. I discuss what events lead me down this path in life to consider a career in naturopathic medicine. I then examine how my four spent in school went there. I outline some of the interesting characters and good friends I met and some of the quirky events that happened there.

There you have it. Here are 18 short stories about my life. They all were true and happened the way I have written about them. Some of them are funny and some are sad. I think all of them are entertaining and interesting. Each one of them has an importance and meaning to me. I hope you enjoy them and find them compelling and engaging too.

CHAPTER 1

Uncle Mickey, the Barber

Mickey Ogloff was a unique character and a fixture of country life in Grand Forks. When I think back about my uncle Mickey, I am reminded by a quote by the 19th century writer and naturalist, Henry David Thoreau. "Why should we be in such desperate haste to succeed and in such desperate enterprises? If a man does not keep pace with his companions, perhaps it is because he hears a different drummer. Let him step to the music which he hears, however measured or far away." He followed the beat of a different drummer and had a simple and inspiring philosophy of life.

Mickey Ogloff was born the youngest of four children to Bill Ogloff and Helen Vatkin in Grand Forks, British Columbia on October 9th, 1923. Mickey's parents were Doukhobors of Russian decent that immigrated to Canada at the turn of the 19th century. They settled in the Nursery area of Grand Forks, just east of the town, where the Kettle River slowly winds it way eastward to Cascade falls. The family farm was just south of the Crowsnest Highway #3 and Candadian Pacific Railway or CPR railway as it left east of Grand Forks. They acquired approximately ten acres just south and east of Nursery Road where the topsoil was rich and fertile. Mickey was born, like most children of this era, at home at the family farm. Mickey had two older sisters, Lola and Elsie and an older brother, Bill. He lived a carefree childhood, working and playing on the family farm and roaming the mountains and streams nearby. It was during these years that he cultivated his deep appreciation and love of nature. It his late teenage years he met Laura Hadiken, a young girl from Manitoba who moved to Grand Forks with her family. After a short courtship Mickey married Laura on July 15, 1944.

Mickey was a farmer. Mickey and his bride settled on the family farm in Nursery and continued farming for a living. It was hard work. They grew wheat and barley. They cultivated apple, pear and plum trees. They grew acres of lettuce just for seed. Sometimes they grew flowers. They grew a variety of grapes and had a small vineyard to make wine.

They had three acres in strawberries. During the summer months Mickey would get up at 5:00 o'clock in the morning and pick fresh strawberries load them on a flatbed truck and go sell them to the local grocery store. They had up to 150 chickens on the farm, several cows including a favourite named Bossy, several horses including a favourite named Prince.

Mickey was a family man. Mickey and Laura had three children; Lanny the oldest, Ronnie the middle child and Rob the youngest. Ronnie was killed in a tragic accident on the family farm. Grandpa Bill, Mickey's dad, was loading apples with tractor and trailer one late summer afternoon on the farm. Ronnie, who was six years old at the time, was crawling over wooden crates on the back trailer despite warnings from Grandpa Bill. When Bill turned the tractor on a steeper slope of the orchard, the crates on the back trailer tipped over and landed on Ronnie. The tragic death forever changed the Ogloff family. Laura was inconsolable for years. Bill forever blamed himself for the accident. And Mickey decided that farming wasn't for him. Laura was already trained as a hair dresser and Mickey decided to go back to school to become a barber.

Mickey was a barber. In 1954, Mickey went to Barber school in Vancouver. After training he returned to Grand Forks and set up his barber shop on Second Street in a small brick building next to the Winnipeg Hotel. Mickey was the town barber for thirty five years. He wore a white jacket at work with pockets in front to hold his scissors and utensils. He was always clean shaven and had has wavy black hair slicked back with brylcream. He had the largest rack of elk antlers on the wall of his barber shop separating his and Laura's rooms. It was the largest antlers that I have ever seen and it over twenty points. There was also lynx, beaver and bear hides on the walls. There was also a stuffed whitetail deer head on the wall staring back at you.

Mickey was a storyteller. I remember as a young child going to his barber shop for a haircut. You would walk in there and look at the pelts and antlers on the wall. The smell of cigarette smoke from Laura's shop would permeate the air. There would be all sorts of people coming and going from the shop. All the town's eccentrics would stop in there at different times. Mickey would be cutting someone's hair with his scissors clipping away and he would be telling a story about the outdoors or about politics or sports. He never would turn anyone away from his shop and always had time to talk to everybody. There was only one barber chair in his shop. He would put a booster seat for me. He would carefully put a plastic smock over me, clip it together at the back of my neck and begin cutting and talking. I would be gazing at the pelts and antlers on the wall,

Uncle Mickey the Barber

wondering where they came from. It was an annual ritual going for hair cuts at my Uncle Mickey's barber shop.

Mickey was a trapper. He had a deep reverence to nature. He enjoyed the outdoors and wanted to teach his sons how to be self-sufficient. The trap line extended from the old Phoenix mine, up the Santa Rosa near Christina Lake to the west side of the Paulson summit. At its prime he had nineteen cabins on the trap line. During the winter months, Mickey used to go snowshoeing on the trap line. He would work Tuesday to Saturday at the barber shop and have Sundays and Mondays off to explore the outdoors. He would trap mink, muskrats, weasels, beavers, lynx and occasionally cougars and skunks.

Mickey was an avid outdoorsman. He would go moose hunting in the Caribou region and go elk hunting in the East Kootenays. He would go fishing for sturgeon in the Columbia River near Castlegar and for walleye in the Pend o'reille River by Trail. In the late summer of 1976, he loaded up his old red Dodge pickup truck and put on a camper and with his wife Laura drove to the Yukon and Alaska. Never in a rush to get to their destination they would camp and fish along the way. They went to Whitehorse and Dawson City and even went as far as the Arctic Circle on the Dempster Highway. At this point it was getting cold and late and he borrowed some gas from another forlorn traveller on the Dempster, turned around and came back home.

Mickey was pragmatic. Growing up in the Great Depression taught him to economize, re-use and keep things for a rainy day. He wouldn't throw away things. He had several barns and buildings on the farm on Nursery Road. They were full of stuff including nails, hammers and building materials to canned goods and wood. He stored up to sixty cords of wood on the farm that he would burn himself during winter or sell to others. He made his own wine, canned his fruit, made his own bullets and gun shells, cured his own meat and tanned his own hides. He was self-sufficient and practical and had good financial acumen.

Mickey was compassionate. He loved animals, especially dogs and was particularly fond of golden labs. He wasn't original and named his first lab Goldie. After this lab passed away, he got another lab and named her Goldie. After this lab passed he got another lab and named her Goldie. At one time he had eight dogs and thirteen cats on the farm. People would drop off stray cats at the farm after the young kittens become not so cute. Mickey fed and cared for the cats because they would catch all the mice that were in the barns. In later years, Mickey got two toy

14

poodles and named them Pierre and Baptiste. He spoiled the two poodles and many times Mickey was seen driving his old Buick car with Laura sitting in the back seat and Pierre and Baptiste sitting next to him in the front seat.

Mickey was generous. In the fall Mickey would get seven hundred pounds of cull potatoes. He would take the potatoes back to his farm and store them over winter. In the cold winter months he would cut up a large bucket of the potatoes and then spread them over one of his fields. Hungry whitetail and mule deer would appear and eat the potatoes. On the coldest days there would be thirty to forty hungry deer eating potatoes. By the end of the winter the appreciative deer would become tame and almost eat out of his hand.

Mickey showed acts of civil disobedience. He stood up for what he believed was right. On one occasion he was transporting a load of cedar shingles through downtown Grand Forks. The load was uncovered and some of the shingles fell off onto to the road. A young police constable pulled Mickey over and issued him a ticket for his alleged offence. Mickey refused to pay the fine and he went to court in Grand Forks. The judge said that he should pay the fine and write a check. Mickey said he didn't have any checks. The judge said that he should pay the fine in cash. Mickey said he didn't have any cash on him. The judge rescinded the thirty dollar fine and Mickey was allowed to walk out of court a free man.

Mickey was an agnostic. It wasn't so much that he didn't believe in God, as it was his dissatisfaction with organized religion of the time. He didn't believe in the afterlife and didn't follow the dogma of orthodox beliefs. Breaking away from his Russian Doukhobor ancestry, Mickey wasn't vegetarian, ate meat, was a trapper, owned guns and shot wild game for food. He didn't hesitate to explain his beliefs when other people tested his faith. Mickey was well read. He would spend many evenings reading in his living room in an old reclining chair in front of his fireplace surrounded by bear hides on the floor. He was well read and could converse on a wide variety of topics.

Mickey was a craftsman and a marksman. He liked to go to black powder shoots in Kettle Falls, silhouette shoots in Colville and turkey shoots in Midway. Mickey made his own bullets and gun shells. He made beautiful knives with handles carved from deer antlers that he collected on the trap line. He enjoyed watching Indian celebrations at the banks of the Columbia River. It was while returning from a trip Spokane that a humorous, but dangerous event occurred. While driving slowly homeward, north of Chewelah, some young youths in a car passed him and Laura. They immediately slowed down and played chicken with the much older Mickey. The allowed Mickey to pass them and then sped up, passed him, slowed down and played chicken with him again. This went on for some time till the young yahoos were again passing Mickey. Mickey reached under his seat, pulled out an unloaded hand gun that he had brought to the gun show. He brandished it in the window. The hoodlums were immediately mortified by such a display of firearm by the old man. They quickly sped away and were never seen again.

Mickey didn't follow fashion trends. He would dress the way he wanted to and wasn't influenced by anybody else's opinion including Laura's. When he wasn't at work Mickey dressed like a farmer. He would dress in overalls and wear a big, floppy straw hat. One summer, Mickey and Laura went to a party in Castlegar. Laura could not influence his decision of what to wear. In the summer heat he showed up wearing wool pants and a plaid flannel shirt. I remember going to the provincial park at the south end of Christina Lake in summer. Laura would be sitting in her summer attire on a lawn chair in the shade on the grass strip before the sandy public beach. Mickey would be lying on the ground wearing his overalls on, his large straw hat and big boots on. He would chew a blade of grass between his teeth, enjoying the moment and revelling in the natural beauty around him.

Mickey changed with the times. He sold the farm on Nursery Road in 1991 and moved to downtown Grand Forks. He built a beautiful house just south of the Co-op building near City Park right against the Kettle River. Every winter Mickey would buy six sacks of grain. Each morning he would stand at a slow portion of the river that buttressed against his property and throw out handfuls of grain to ducks that swam in the waters near the shore. At first there were only one or two ducks. By the end of the winter there were one hundred and fifty appreciative ducks that fed on grain from Mickey's hand. One of his sons suggested to Mickey that they should have roasted duck for dinner. Mickey said he would have none of that and that they were all his pets.

Mickey was irreverent. When his sister Elsie's daughter, Betty got married Mickey gave the couple a bear skin for a wedding present. When Elsie passed away, they had her remains cremated and scattered over the south side of Rattlesnake Mountain. One of the relatives flew a small plane and flew over the mountain. A small group of relatives, including Mickey and Betty congregated near the old homestead site near Highway #3. After Elsie's ashes had been scattered a bald eagle was seen soaring down over the exact site where this occurred. Some of the relatives looking on by the road said this was a religiously symbolic. Mickey disagreed and explained that there was probably a dead dear carcass there and the eagle was going to feed.

Uncle Mickey taught me to work hard to get what you want. Work honestly and respectfully and you would feel good about yourself. Don't always be in a hurry to get where you're going. And of course, think for yourself. Like Thoreau's classic quote, Uncle Mickey followed the beat of a different drummer. Mickey Ogloff passed away in Grand Forks May 19, 2003.

CHAPTER 2

Bobby and Me

I grew up in Grand Forks, British Columbia with the rest of my family. I was born into a traditional family with a mother and father and two brothers and a sister. We lived in a house in this small town and shared many memories with each other. We grew up together and mostly nourished and supported each other. We were imperfect, jagged and rough at times. We survived and adapted and did the best we could. We were still a family.

Bobby was my oldest brother. Robert Allen Lobay (Vatkin) was born November 18, 1953 to Marion and Walter Vatkin. He was my biological half-brother. My mother Marion was married before to Walter Vatkin. They had two children named Bobby and Jim. Walter drowned in a fishing accident in his late twenties. My mother then met and married my dad George in 1964. They had two child named Arlene and myself, Doug. My dad George adopted Bobby and Jim and raised them as his own. He was fair and honest and loved them as much as he loved me and my sister. There was no distinction between us and we were all George and Marion's children

Bobby and I had a special relationship. Conversely, Jim and my younger sister Arlene also had a close relationship. Bobby was my older brother by 11 years. He used to babysit all the children. He cooked for us, played with us and helped us do things. He used to buy use toys, candy and other things. He dropped us off at school and picked us up again when it was time to go home. Bobby used to bundle me with a blanket on the couch when we watched television together. I remember dreaming that I was on a magic carpet flying gently through the air. Bobby used to carry me downstairs when I was falling asleep and carry me back upstairs to my bedroom. He was a bigger older brother who nourished and protected me. He loved me and I loved him.

When Bobby was 18 years old my parents bought him a hot red GT Fastback Mustang car with side markers and a spoiler on the back. It was a high performance powerful car with a big 4.7 litre v-8 engine. It probably had too much power for an inexperienced high school student. He was working at the local Pope and Talbot Sawmill part-time on evenings and weekends. He was finishing grade 12 and was getting ready to graduate high school. He did well at school and was planning to go to college to study Forestry. He had a beautiful blond girlfriend named Mona, who was also his graduation date. His future looked bright and rosy.

Jim was my older brother and Bobby's younger brother. Jim was 7 years older than me and was born on July 1957. He was short and slim with dirty brown hair and brown eyes. Jim was fairly smart, but didn't apply himself in school. He liked drafting and math and didn't care for his other classes. He graduated from school and did average in his studies. He had had some less than honourable friends who lead him astray. In high school he started to party and drink alcohol and use other stuff. I remember when he was in grade 10, he told my mother that his cannabis plant in our garden was a teacher mandated science experiment. My mother believed him.

Jim introduced me to rock music of the 1970's. I remember listening to the tunes of AC/DC, Alice Cooper, Aerosmith, Deep Purple and Led Zeppelin. It was a time of long hair, bell bottoms and a lot of incense. Somehow through it all, Jim convinced my parents to buy him a silver Chevrolet Camaro. Now he had a hot car to go parties with and party he did. I remember going out on weekends returning home late at night or many times early in the morning. I also remember returning from family trips with my parents when Jim was allowed to stay home. The house would smell of cigarettes and beer cans. After talking to our neighbors it was confirmed that Jim had a very large party with cars lined up for blocks. Sometimes a policeman would show up at door bring Jim home or issue a citation. Either way he found his fair share of trouble. Of course my parents tried to stop and discourage him.

Jim had a stubborn streak and it was like two mountain goats bumping heads. I remember walking down Central Avenue on Boxing Day when a policeman pulled over and picked him up for an outstanding warrant. I remember another time in a case of mistaken identity he was an unwitting accomplice in an armed robbery. Talk about being in the wrong place at the wrong time. In this untimely affair he was asked by the perpetrator of a crime for a ride after the incident. He unknowingly and innocently gave the perpetuator a ride after the crime and inadvertently helped the criminal escape. With all his experiences Jim could probably write a useful manual for teenagers of things not to do and what to do if you do. After graduation, he decided to move away from home to Calgary and pursue a career in surveying technology. He did ok.

Arlene was my younger sister by one year. She was born February 1966. She was the only girl in a family of boys and she was the youngest. She had blond hair and blue eyes. She was smart but not quite as smart as her older brother, but she did very well in school. She was however, a better athlete. She played a diverse group of sports and excelled at them all. She was strong and fast. When I was in hockey, she was in figure skating. I remember my mom always sewing sequin-laced dresses for ice carnivals and other skating competitions. She used to skate in pairs with a young boy from Danville, Washington named Scott. He was orphaned along with his sister Kelly and were raised by their grandmother Dorothy. She was a nice lady and I remember spending a lot of time at their house across the border. Arlene also excelled at many other sports including basketball, softball and volleyball. She also travelled a lot with her sports teams. I think sports was her way of escaping from the family. She was perhaps more sensitive than boys and things seemed to affect her more. After graduation she attended BCIT or the British Columbia Institute of Technology and pursued a career in business. She was married for a while, had one lovely daughter and moved back to Grand Forks.

George was my dad. He was the hunter gatherer and strong silent type. He was the bread winner of the family. He worked as a shop foreman at the Ministry of Transportation and Highways. He was a skilled mechanic and a quasi, jack of all trades. He could weld and fabricate things and he did some carpentry, electrical and plumbing. He built three wheeled recreational vehicles, motorized go-karts and snowmobiles. He was avid outdoorsman and sportsman. He loved the outdoors and enjoyed hunting and getting firewood. He was practical and pragmatic.

Marion was my mother. She was of Russian Doukhobor ancestry. Her parents were Bill and Mary Kurnoff. She was born in May 9, 1933 and grew up in Grand Forks, British Columbia. She was raised in the

Doukhobor community on Hardy Mountain on a bluff overlooking the town with her brother Mike. She first married Walter Vatkin when she was 19 years old. Together they had two children named Bobby and Jim. Walter was killed in a drowning accident when she was 29 years old. She was widowed and had two young boys to raise. She met my father George when she was in her early 30's. They fell in love and had a whirlwind romance. They were married in 1964. Together they had two children Doug and my sister Arlene. We were a family of four children including Bobby, Jim, Arlene and myself.

Marion was an avid homemaker and gardener. She enjoyed staying at home and raising her family. She did all the cooking and cleaning and she basically ran the household while my dad was at work. She cooked all types of meals including Russian food and contemporary Canadian cuisine. She particularly liked cooking borscht and eating food directly from our organic garden. She was skilled at sewing and knitting. She sewed clothes and outfits and knitted blankets and sweaters. She liked gardening in our big garden in the back of the yard at our house. She didn't drive because she had an auto accident in her early 20's and never renewed her license. She was dependent on my dad to drive and get groceries in town. She enjoyed talking on the phone to her friends and relatives in both Russian and English. She also liked socializing and talking with her friends at our house. I remember her sitting around the dining room table or outside on our balcony with her husband and many other friends and relatives including Jane, Lucy, Alec and Marilyn, Mickey and Laura, Mike and Annette and Nick and Helen. They would talk for hours about religion, politics and anything else. They would have coffee or tea, snacks and lunch or dinner and then talk and socialize some more. There was usually a lot of laughter and sometimes some heated debates and discussions. There always seemed to be people coming and going from our house at various times. Marion liked to watch funny shows on television. Her favorite shows were All in the Family, Sanford and Son, Three's Company and Seinfeld. She also liked reading and particularly enjoyed reading the bible. Her favorite chapter in the bible was the poetic book of Psalms.

We lived on an acre of land located on a flood plain in west Grand Forks, on 17th street just before a hill on Central Avenue going over the train tracks. The soil was a rich, black earth that was fertile and excellent for farming. We grew a big organic garden of fresh fruits and vegetables

21

each year. We harvested beans, cabbage, carrots, corn, cucumbers, lettuce, potatoes, and tomatoes. Our house was a big, sprawling rancher with a basement. There were three bedrooms upstairs and one bedroom in the basement. We had a root cellar and a cold storage room for food and preserves. We had a gas furnace and also a large wood stove my dad had fabricated in the basement. We always used the wood stove in winter time to heat the house along with the gas furnace. I can remember spending many nights in front of the wood stove after returning from playing hockey at the arena. My body was aching and tired and I would sprawl out in front of the warm inviting fire. I would lay out my equipment nearby and fall asleep. I would stoke the stove with pieces of dry larch. I would watch the flames dance around as the first crackled away. The deep, relaxing warmth of the fire was incredible. The infrared heat emitted by the stove would penetrate deep in my body like a hot drink. Sometimes I would wake up sweating. The fire from the stove was always lubricating, healing and refreshing. For the most part, our home was a busy, friendly and happy place.

I used to walk about three blocks to Perley Elementary School. I crossed over a bare field behind Holoboffs and the Tastee Tree Restaurant on a well-worn path. My mother would pack a lunch and I would go off in the morning. I liked to go to school, play with my friends and learn about new things. On the way back home I would return on the same path. I remember hearing crickets chirping and grasshoppers clicking away all along path which was bordered by waist high dry grass and knapweed. Many times I could smell the fragrant aroma of my mom's fresh bread wafting in the air. I couldn't wait to get home after school and lather a fresh slice of bread with butter and a chunk of cheese. My favorite sandwich when I was young was cucumber and cheese. I would always look forward to staying home when I was sick and having my cheese and cucumber sandwich and watching Sesame Street.

Home life was busy, full and rich. My dad worked full time and doing mechanics for odd jobs and working on his home improvement projects. My mom was the matriarch and homemaker making sure our household was running relatively smoothly. Our front door was open and revolving for most of the day. Four of us kids of different ages were coming and going at various times with school and activities. My brothers and I played hockey and my sister took figure skating lessons. We spent a lot of time at the arena and travelling to different games and tournaments.

The older boys generally looked after themselves and my parents helped the younger kids. The same was true for school. My brothers walked to school when they were younger and drove themselves when they were older.

One day in June of 1972 when my brother Bobby was 19 years old that all changed. I remember there was first a knock and then somebody rang our doorbell late on Sunday night. It was a police officer dressed in uniform with yellow pin stripped pants, a badge on his jacket and a wide, brimmed hat. My dad invited him inside. In a somber tone of voice the police officer told my parents that my brother Bobby was killed, along with his best friend Johnny, in an auto accident in Kaleden, just south of Penticton. In a moment of incredulity there was then crying, sobbing and wailing. Shortly thereafter there was a large funeral at the USCC Russian community complex. Things in our family seemed to change forever after this.

My mother became disinterested in conforming to the normal activities of society. After a period of initial shock and grief there was then a time of deep contemplation and soul searching. She began to read the bible in earnest and study with different religious groups. She settled with a contemporary Christian group that didn't follow conventional beliefs. We stopped celebrating Christmas and questioned the Sunday Sabbath. We studied the bible but never really went to church afterwards. During this time my dad became detached and indifferent to mom's new beliefs. My older brother Jim became a disillusioned and unsettled teenager.

Life went on, but in a different way. The unexpected death of a child and a brother had a profound effect on our family. There was a long period of bereavement marked by episodes of disbelief, anger, anxiety and depression. It was also followed by a time of deep contemplation, meditation and reflection. I was seven years old when this traumatic event occurred. I was too young to understand the full implications of my brother's passing, but still felt its effects. I only knew that Bobby wasn't around anymore and I missed him. I still went to school, played sports, socialized with friends and did all the other things I was supposed to do.

I spent more time at my grandmother's place a few blocks away on 18th Street. She was my mom's mother named Mary Kurnoff and who

23

was widowed. She had a small, clean house with a bathroom just off the kitchen. My grandmother was a beautiful lady who cooked, dressed and told me wonderful stories. She had a big veranda and two big maple trees in the front of house. In autumn the leaves would change to the colours of watermelon red, apricot orange and lemon yellow. I would rake the leaves into a huge pile and splash around in there for hours with my friends. Ian and Jeff lived across the street. I used to go there to play and have lunch sometimes. David lived on the next street over with his brothers and sisters in a big, old house. As far as I knew he didn't have a dad around and was raised by his mother. His family atmosphere was wild and free. I used to go over there to play in the dirt with little hot wheel cars with him. I had a lot of fun at my grandmothers and the memory of my older brother's passing faded.

Like the anachronistic euphemism, life goes on. What can you do? Do your best and keep going on. Life has a way of teaching you something. I think the main thing I learnt from this affair is that life is transient and unpredictable. You can't predict what is going to happen next. In is not healthy to ruminate and dwell on the past. The past is gone and is not coming back. Conversely, it not wise to worry and to get anxious about the future. You have no control of the future to a large degree. All you can do is live in the present moment to your best ability and enjoy the day. Carpe diem, seize the day.

CHAPTER 3

George the mechanic

My dad George was a skilled mechanic. He fixed things, primarily machinery, equipment and automobiles. He was also a technician, a repairman, an engineer and a serviceman. My dad was all of those and more. He was skilled and proficient auto mechanic. He was a craftsman and an artisan. He was an inventor and an innovator. He was proficient in welding, machining, carpentry, electrical and plumbing. He was a jack of all trades. He was an avid outdoorsman and sportsman. He was patient and stoical. He was practical and pragmatic. He was quiet and aloof. He was kind and humble. He was proud man who also had faults and flaws. He was the archetypical hunter gatherer. He was a man's man of years gone by.

George Paul Lobay was born January 20, 1929 in Kobrin, Poland which is now a part of Belorussia. He was the only child of Paul and Anastasia Lobay. His family immigrated to Canada in the fall of 1937 just before the outbreak of World War II. I remember asking him what he remembered about his past as he was leaving Eastern Europe and moving to Canada. Without hesitation, he said seeing acres and acres of tanks and artillery in Germany as the train he was on was passing through to France and then Britain. His family settled in Innisfail, Alberta when they arrived in Canada. They moved to Grand Forks, British Columbia in 1945 and had a small farm on Carson Road. George began working for the Ministry of Transportation and Highways in 1947. He worked and apprenticed as a mechanic then as a shop foreman. He married Marion Kurnoff in 1964. Together they raised four children, Robert, James, Doug and Arlene. He was predeceased by his son Bobbie in 1972. He had three grandchildren Rachel and Jessica of Kelowna and Christina of Grand Forks. He was a skillful mechanic and avid outdoorsman. He enjoyed hunting, getting wood and sports including hockey and wrestling.

Uncle Mickey the Barber

George was a big stocky man and stood 5 foot 11 inches in height in his prime. He was muscular and very strong physically. He had big biceps, a wide round barrel chest and thick legs. He could lift an automobile engine with his bare hands and chop and saw wood with reckless abandon. He would work in his garage shop in the cold of winter and be lifting and moving heavy tools and material. He had Slavic facial features with a square face, dark, slicked back hair, an angular jaw and, sharp chin and a nose with a hump in the middle. He had thick hands that were pretty nimble for a big man. He had features of his blended Russian, Polish and Ukrainian descent.

George completed Grade 13 at Grand Forks Secondary School in Grand Forks. He did well in most of his classes and he particularly liked social studies and sciences. He said he wanted to be a dentist. He was also interested in mechanics. He liked to take things apart, tinker with them and then put them back together. He got a job at the Department of Highways in Grand Forks when he was 18 years old. He apprenticed as a junior mechanic and enjoyed the work. He became a shop foreman at the Grand Forks operation and worked in management for the remainder of his career. He worked a total of 42 years at the Ministry of Highways until his retirement in 1988. He went to Victoria shortly after his retirement to receive a citation and gold watch for many years of service from the premier Bill Bennett. When I graduated from Bastyr College in 1991 he gave me his engraved Swiss Omega gold watch as a present. I have kept it as a memento and keep sake ever since.

George was a very patient man. He used to take his time and work diligently and proficiently. He would also persevere and had a stick to it attitude. He would often tell me not to give up and hang in there if something wasn't turning out right. He was slow to change things and didn't like to admit defeat. Sometimes this was a good thing and sometimes it was disadvantageous. He didn't like being rushed, but most of the time he worked methodically and efficiently. Sometimes he would get angry if something didn't work out the way he thought it should. He would try again to fix the problem with an analytical and disciplined manner. I would observe him working away for many hours on some mechanical project, whether it was fixing a transmission, taking apart an engine or wiring some house circuits. He taught me to be diligent, disciplined and tenacious.

George, along with other tradesman, built our home on 17th street in 1966. It was a big beautiful rancher on some flat, arable land with good soil but poor drainage. It was located just above a slough and short distance away from Central Avenue towards Observation Mountain. He helped do the carpentry, electrical and plumbing in the house. He was also adept at welding and machining. He would patiently attempt to work at a wide variety of projects. He was willing to learn and he tried hard. If he didn't know something he would sometimes reluctantly ask for help and assistance.

George had an elaborate mechanic shop at home. The mechanic shop was in the garage and the tool shop in our basement. He would fix all sorts of different automobiles including cars, trucks, tractors and lawn mowing machines. He would also attempt to fix small appliances and small electric machines that would break down. He had lifts, compressors, drill presses, table saws and grinders. He had several bright red tool boxes with all sorts of pliers, screw drivers, sockets and wrenches. He also had power tools, oil cans, chain saws and all sorts of useful nick knacks. He had them carefully placed in sequence and order so he would know where to find them. He engraved most of his metallic tools just in case someone borrowed them and failed to give them back. He also had various sorts of mechanical motors, pumps and electrical devices that he might use one day when needed. If I needed a special tool I am sure I would have found it at my dad's shop. If I didn't, he would know where to get it if necessary.

George was an inventor. He liked to build and create things in his shop. He was adept at machining and welding. He built a three wheel off road recreational vehicle before any such machines existed for sale in shops. He also built snowmobiles and go karts for the kids from scratch. He would collect metallic pieces that he needed along with motorized parts and wheels. He would bend, weld and machine these pieces into functional elements. He would assemble and put the parts together to get a working device. He would also adapt and modify existing machines by adding hydraulics, more gears or blades or lifts as in the case of a tractor we had. He did all this with very marginal drawings or plans.

George was a busy mechanic. We had many visitors at our home at all days of the weeks seeking mechanical advice from George. Some people would ask him to do brakes, clutches, rear ends and transfer cases. He worked on all different types of models and makes of cars and trucks.

Uncle Mickey the Barber

He was especially good at diagnosing and fixing the problem when other people failed to find it. Farmers asked him to work on their broken down farm equipment and tractors. He also worked on some big moving trucks, bull dozers and skidders. My mother would get tired and angry at the people showing up and the fact she said George didn't charge much. He sent some people away when he couldn't or didn't want to help them. Some people tried to take advantage of him but that was short lived. He also changed oil and did tire rotations for some widows and relatives. He was honest and reliable.

My dad was my personal mechanic. He did all my mechanical work on my vehicles and my siblings for free. When I was 16 years old he bought me my first car. It was an ugly, purple AMC Gremlin. He would service it, do oil changes, fix broken head lights and change the brakes, gratis. He also let me borrow his light blue GMC truck virtually anytime I wanted. I took the truck with friends to explore the backroads in the mountains around our town, canoeing and rafting and even to outdoor parties late at night. When I went away to Bastyr College in Seattle, Washington, he bought me a stylish, black GMC Blazer sport utility vehicle. It was definitely a step up from the Gremlin. It had a standard transmission with a stick shift on the floor separating the driver and passenger seats. I remember one time in my third year when I was returning home from school at summer, I wasn't able to shift gears. The stick shift was stuck in third gear. At this time I was driving through Manning Park from Vancouver. I didn't know what to do, I had enough gas and decided to keep on driving slowly home to Grand Forks. I made all the way stuck in third gear. My dad realized the transmission was fried. He fixed the problem and replaced the transmission at no charge. I realize now how lucky I was to have a great dad who was my private, personal mechanic.

George was an avid sportsman. When he was young he learned to skate and play hockey. He also learned to box and fight. He was more of a peacemaker and would protect other kids from bullies. He spent a lot of time at billiard halls and was an adroit pool player. He also was interested in flight and took flying lessons at the Grand Forks Airport. He was passionate about hockey and wrestling. I can remember many Saturday evenings at 5 pm when he watched CBC Hockey Night in Canada on the television. We would all crowd around the black and white television in our living room and watch the hockey game with almost religious fervor. He was also fond of wrestling and he would watch those entertaining wrestling shows on the television.

George was a passionate outdoorsman. He loved nature and the outdoors. His favorite television show was an outdoor nature show called Wild Kingdom. He spent a lot of time in the forest and woods around Grand Forks. He loved getting firewood for our wood stove and other relatives and neighbors in need of winter fuel. He would go to places like Phoenix, Pass Creek and Burrell Creek to find suitable birch, larch and pine trees to cut down and buck up. George loved hunting mule and white tail deer in the early fall. He owned several rifles and would practice target shooting at the rifle range. Some of his favorite hunting spots were up the bluffs past May Creek, Pass Creek in the North Fork and the Santa Rosa by Christina Lake. He liked to get up early in the morning with the cool fresh air, frost and autumn sunrise. He also took us fishing at Jewel Lake and Xenia Lake, although he wasn't much of a fisherman. He also took his family huckleberry and mushroom picking. Other times he just liked to go for a ride in his old truck and just look at the natural beauty all around.

George had a quiet personality by nature. He wasn't as gregarious or loquacious as some people. Mom said he was like this because he was an only child and an immigrant who didn't speak English when he arrived. He had to adapt and learn the language as best as he could. Maybe it was some sort of coping mechanism. He was more introspective and thoughtful. He said what needed to be said and moved on. He preferred working on mechanical projects in focused attentiveness than have idle chatter some people. He would socialize when visitors came over and he was more affable when he was talking about something he liked. He enjoyed doing things more than he liked talking about them.

George was kind-hearted and he meant well. He was humble and never talked about himself much. He wouldn't brag or boast about his accomplishments and he wouldn't dwell on his failures. He had pride and was a proud man, but he wouldn't gloat about things he did. He treated all animals and pets with compassion and respect. I remember many times him gently caressing our pet dog Frisky and Chico or carefully helping them down from the back of the truck to the ground. Even when he was hunting he had a kind reverence for the animals he was pursuing. He never really yelled at his children, even when we were doing something wrong or bad. He didn't really swear or cuss. I only heard him shout expletives when something was going wrong on his mechanical projects, or he was mad at his wife. One time he had removed a car engine on a hoist and had placed it on a makeshift table with saw horses. He had been working for hours on this project and the engine suddenly fell to the ground. He yelled, exchanged some expletives, took a break and picked up the pieces of the project and moved on.

George had character flaws and imperfections like the rest of humanity. He was sometimes aloof and distant. A counsellor might say he had communication difficulties. He had difficulty communicating with my mother. She was loquacious and talkative. He was quiet and reserved. He had trouble showing and sharing his emotions. He kept things inside and only rarely shared his feelings about things. I knew he loved his wife and family, but he only showed his deep seated feelings on rare occasions. He would rather work and putter, than focus on feelings and emotions. He also had a stubborn streak and he was recalcitrant and head strong. He was used to working independently. He was the expert mechanic and usually people asked him for his advice. He was the shop foreman and boss at work. He had trouble giving in, asking for advice and admitting failure.

George also had a woodchuck in his woodpile. He had an addiction and dependency to alcohol. He was an alcoholic. It is still hard for me to admit this. Looking back I think he had a genetic predisposition to this problem. When he was younger and working, he would drink after work sometimes and on the weekend. While working he seemed to be able to control his fermented liquid consumption. After he retired when he was 60 years old, his addiction got the better of him. It affected our family dynamics. Although his relationship with my mother was tempered at the best of times, this made it worse. He would drink and they would argue. I think he would drink sometimes because they did argue. He was a proud and stubborn man and had difficulty admitting he had a problem. He would leave the house and go outside to his shop or to the woodshed. He would also leave to go out elsewhere. A lot of times he went back out into the backwoods and the comfort of nature. I think he found some peace and solace there.

George loved old time music. We used to have a large, bulky record player that was cumbersome and heavy to move. He had a collection of records dating back to the 1950's. On many Saturday nights he would play his favorite records. He loved Lara's Theme from the classic show Doctor Zhivago about a Russian doctor and his love during the Bolshevik Revolution. He would also play records from Andy Williams, Dean Martin, Lois Armstrong and Nat King Cole. Sometimes my mother and he would even waltz together to the music in the background. The music he played still resonates with me today. I play guitar music and sing in old folk's homes, retirement complexes and coffee shops. Much of the music I play are the songs that I heard when I was young. I have three songs that remind me of my dad. I play Leader of the Band by Dan Folgerberg and Old Man and Needle and the Damage by Neil Young. They remind me of my father and my relationship with him. Coincidentally, I have trouble picking a song about my mother. The only song I could come up with is Bad Moon Rising by Creedence Clearwater Revival. In her religious fervour she would always say the end of the world is coming soon.

My dad George was a good man in many ways. He was a great father and he provided for his family as best as he could. We were never without food or clothes and always had cars and the best sports equipment. He had some exemplary characteristics such as patience and diligence. He taught me to persevere, work hard and to stick to it. He was a skilled mechanic and gifted tradesman. He taught me to love and respect the outdoors and natural world around us. He also had his character flaws and imperfections like the rest of us. He was my dad, the mechanic. He passed away at home on Sunday June 13, 2010.

CHAPTER 4

Uncle Mike From Castlegar

Mike Kurnoff was my mother's older brother who lived in Castlegar, British Columbia. He was born in Grand Forks on January 12, 1929. He lived and was raised with his family in the Doukhobor village settlement near Hardy Mountain in west Grand Forks. His family lived in a two story brick house on a bluff overlooking Ward Lake, Observation Mountain and the western stretch of the Sunshine Valley. They had chickens, cows and grew their vegetables in a big garden and gathered fruit from trees on their land. He would walk to school and downtown Grand Forks for errands and shopping. He married Annette Zubcoff when he was 20 years old on January 18, 1949. Together they had three daughters named Violet, Lisa and Carol. Times were tough after the end of World War II and the great depression and he took what work he could. He travelled to the Okanagan to work as a fruit picker and in a packing house. He worked as a carpenter. He worked for Ferraro's Grocery Store in Trail, B.C. He also worked for C.P. Rail as a train engineer.

My first recollection of Uncle Mike was when the Canadian Pacific or C.P. train would come to town. The rail tracks were just a short distance up the hill away from our house. Mom would tell me that Uncle Mike was coming to town and he would be driving the train. I would scurry up to the railways and patiently wait on the side of the tracks. I would hear the distant whistle of the approaching train echo in the valley. I would put several copper pennies on the top of the tracks and wait for the heavy train to press them flat. The train would pass by and I would be careful to stand back at a distance and watch. Mike would lean out of the side of locomotive car and wave. He wore a striped conductor hat with denim overalls and gloves. He would toot the horn of the train several times in succession as he passed by, just to acknowledge me and give me a thrill. I smiled and waved. After the train passed by I would pick up my flattened pennies and go home.

When Mike worked for Ferraro's Grocery Store and during the early part of his career for C.P. Rail he lived for several years on the hillside in Trail, B.C. Trail was famous for the large mining and smelting company called Cominco. There was a large industrial complex with tall smoke stacks on the side of the hills going up towards Rossland. Of course Trail was famous for winning the world championship of hockey in 1961. The Trail Smoke Eaters was the last independent senior men's hockey team to ever complete such a feat. Trail was a strong sporting town and still produces many top quality hockey and baseball players. I happened to be born in Trail when my parents were visiting Mike and Annette during New Year's Eve on January 1, 1965. Mike used to smoke a pipe which was fashionable at that time. When I was about five years old there was a picture of me dressed in a suit. I had Uncle Mike's pipe in my mouth and my arms around two little friends.

Mike retired from Ferraro's but continued to work for C.P Rail. He moved his family to Castlegar. Our family would make many routine trips through the mountains and over the Paulson Summit to Castlegar to go visit Mike, Annette and their family. We looked forward to the trips and we would load up our car and head over on a Saturday or Sunday. They lived on 4th avenue in the Kinnaird subdivision of Castlegar. They had a small, clean and tidy house overlooking the Columbia River from the west on the high steep bluffs. They had a veranda in the back of their house with a beautiful view of the river to the east. Annette would cook scrumptious meals and serve lunch on the veranda. We would sit, talk and eat the food and imbue the view of the Doukhobor settlement called Ooteschenia across and the river below. It was a beautiful setting and the company and the food was good too.

Mike was a gifted talker. He was garrulous and gregarious. He could talk about anything. He made you feel comfortable. He was knowledgeable. He seemed interested and asked you questions. He would listen to you attentively and then he would give good advice when asked. He was a popular and frequent speaker at weddings, funerals and other events. I remember one time Mike was the speaker at an A.A. or Alcoholics Anonymous meeting held in the basement of some church in Castlegar. I was young at the time and he invited me to go with him. All the people there seemed to know Mike. He attracted people like a magnet. Many people came up to shake his hand, say hello and ask him how things were going. Mike would be attentive and he would greet them all the same. He treated everybody equally and made them feel important. Mike gave his speech and talked up about his struggles with his addiction to alcohol. He was proud to be sober for over 20 years. People listened closely. Mike would often use humour when he was talking. To this day I remember the joke he used in his talk. He said, some drunk was attending an A.A. meeting and sat in the back listening to a speaker. The speaker brought out a bottle of vodka and poured the spirits in a glass along with a glass of water. The speaker brought out two earthworms. He placed one of the worms in the glass of water and the other worm in the glass of vodka. The worm in the glass of water just wriggled around. The worm in the glass of vodka dissolved and disintegrated. The speaker then asked the audience what the moral of this story was. The half inebriated drunk in the back put up his hand and answered. He said the way he understood it, if you drink vodka you will never get worms. The crowd listening to Mike roared with laughter.

Mike used to drink and smoke too much. When his children were young he would often go out drinking after work. The demands of work and family put a strain on his relationship with Annette. Alcohol seemed to numb things and make it better for a while. It would help him relax and ease his pains and demons. Annette sent an ultimatum to him. It was either drinking or family. In one of his drunken stupors she took a bottle and broke it over his head. That seemed to do the trick and awaken him. He quit drinking and smoking. He joined AA or Alcoholics Anonymous. He was a lifelong member of this organization and was a chapter president for many years. He counselled and supported many friends and peers when they had trouble. He had over 45 years of sobriety.

When I was young, it was my lifelong dream to go to Disneyland. I had a map of Disneyland on the wall of my bedroom. It was supposed to be a magical and enchanted place for kids from all over the world. I knew all the different regions of the theme park and all the rides I wanted to go on. These places included the Haunted House, Pirates of the Caribbean, Space Mountain and the Matterhorn. When I was 11 years old our family decided to take a road trip to Disneyland in Anaheim, California. Mike, Annette and his daughter Carol would also go on the trip. We would drive there. We loaded up our old Ford L.T.D. car and headed south to the United States along with Mike and his family. Mike was a natural born leader. He drove his car, led the way and we followed.

He studied the maps, asked for directions and maneuvered elegantly down the Interstate Highway I-5 and freeways of Los Angeles. We made it there in 3 days, had a wonderful time in Disneyland and visited my mom's aunt in Mission Viejo.

Mike loved sports. He especially loved hockey, baseball and golf. He used to watch National Hockey League or N.H.L. hockey on CBC every Saturday night. He also liked watching football. He loved golf and was a long time member at the Castlegar Golf Club. He would talk about his clubs, his swing, his handicap and his score. Friends would often phone him at home during our visits asking him to golf. He would golf several times during the week during golf season. He would often take me golfing when we were visiting. Everybody seemed to know him at the golf course and would come up to say hello to him. He owned a golf cart that he stored at the club. He would let me drive the golf car when we were playing. He gave me a set of clubs to use and encouraged me while we were playing. I was young, didn't know much about golf and didn't have the propensity or patience to play properly. It was still fun going with him. When I was in Selkirk College for one year when I was 19 years old, he encouraged me to take winter golf lessons to improve my stroke and game. Looking back now those lessons helped me a lot. I credit Mike with teaching me how to play this game with some semblance of adequacy.

When I was 13 and 14 years old I played hockey and made many trips to play teams in Castlegar. Mike would come out and watch many of the games. He cheered me on and supported me. He encouraged me and gave me advice to improve my game. I remember one time we were playing in a midget tournament in Castlegar. I thought I was a pretty good hockey player. I was big, strong and had good hands. I used to play centre and score a fair amount of goals. However, at this tournament I was struggling and not playing to my potential. I was a little uptight and nervous. Mike suggested that I relax a little and try not to take things so seriously. It was okay to make mistakes and have fun. During one of the later games he gave a glass of wine before the game to loosen up a bit. I play one of my best games, scored three goals and was the first star for my team that game.

In summer, my mother would send me to stay at the Kurnoff's for a week at a time. They accepted me with open arms and treated me well. I would do chores around the house like mowing the lawn, weeding the garden and cleaning windows. I slept in the basement and they fed me well. They would have visitors over and we would talk and play cards. Mike took me to the golf course and they took me swimming at Syringa Creek. I remember one Sunday they took me for a drive north to Slocan, Silverton and New Denver. We explored the old ghost town of Sandon and then back home to Castlegar. On another trip we went Ainsworth Hot Springs and soaked in the warm mineral water overlooking Kootenay Lake. We stopped in Balfour and visited some of their old friends. There I learned about family history, genealogy and tracing family tree. It was fun and exciting to travel and visit places and people with Mike and Annette.

Mike loved to read. He would read books and magazine on a many different subjects. This helped make him knowledgeable and well rounded. He could converse on many different topics including politics, religion, sports and just about anything else. I remember many times he would sit on his lazy boy chair in his living room with a book or newspaper. Sometimes he wouldn't agree with you and he would vocalize his opinion. He also had a temper and if he felt you were wrong, he certainly would let you know. He particularly liked sports biographies and learning about his favorite sports heroes. When I was in college we used to exchange books about hockey players like Gordie Howe, Bobby Orr and Ken Dryden. We would often talk on the phone about the books and players after we read them.

Mike and Annette would often come to Grand Forks for a visit. They would visit with my parents at our dining room table and have coffee, tea and lunch. They sometimes played cards and sang old Russian hymns. They would laugh, argue and scold each other. When he would show up at our house he was always groomed and well dressed. Many times he would wear a suit, clean shirt, tie and polished shoes. He looked smart and distinguished. When I was a teenage he encouraged me to dress appropriately. He told me to have some respect and dress properly. He told me to wear a belt with my pants and wear dark socks with dark shoes and dark slacks. He taught me how to tie a tie.

Mike was an incredible family man and husband. He was married to Annette for over 64 years. He was very nurturing and supportive to all his children and grandchildren. Family was of the upmost importance to him. I am sure like any married couple that had their ups and downs and share of good times and not so good times. They stuck together through thick and thin. I remember looking him up on google once. There was a picture of him and Annette celebrating their 60th wedding anniversary in 2009 in a C.P. Railway magazine. Together they raised three daughters named Violet, Lisa and Carol. He showered them with love. He regularly talked to them on the phone and would visit them in places they moved to like Edmonton and Okotoks, Alberta. He led by example and set a standard of behavior. He showed what it was like to be a good father and husband. I learned from him. I tried to emulate him when I got married and had children too.

Mike had a heart attack when he was 44 years old. He was working for C.P. Railway and had the stresses of growing teenage family. His doctor told him to quit smoking, change his diet and exercise more. His dad Bill also had heart disease and succumbed to a heart attack at the age of 50 years. A specialist in Vancouver recommended cardiac bypass surgery. At this time bypass surgery was in its infancy and was a risky procedure. Mike was getting chest pains and angina. I remember my mom was extremely worried about him and the surgery. We spent many times praying for his health and safety. His chest was cut open, he was put on life support and had five vascular grafts inserted to supply his heart with oxygen. He made major changes to his lifestyle and diet and continued to live a healthy life. He slowly recovered and healed.

Uncle Mike was an important part of my youth. He was a model of adulthood and personage to emulate. He was a distinguished gentleman. He was always sharp and well dressed. He was genuine and kind hearted. He was always encouraging and comforting. He was very personable. He was always informative and talkative. He would listen and give advice when appropriate. He set the standards and behaviours to strive for. He reminded me of Joe Dimaggio of baseball fame and Jean Beliveau of hockey fame who played for the Montreal Canadians. Mike Kurnoff passed away peacefully at Kootenay Boundary Regional Hospital on Thursday, July 18, 2013, blessed with 84 years of life. Uncle Mike was a wise, cool old guy

CHAPTER 5

Hockey, Saddle Lake and the Big, Bad Bruins

All I really needed to know about life, I learned in peewee house hockey. Hockey has been an integral part of my life since I was a young child. I remember learning to skate on our backyard skating rink for hours. I watched NHL or National Hockey League games on television. I played atom, peewee, bantam and midget hockey in the minor hockey association in our community. I practiced and played games with intense and passionate fervor. I worked on skating, stickhandling, passing and shooting skills over and over again. I played shinny games. In winter, I skated and played hockey on frozen ponds. In summer, I played road hockey with my friends for hours. I imagined I was some famous hockey star and I tried to emulate the way they played. I collected hockey cards and read hockey magazines. I followed and watched the junior B hockey team in our town. I played hockey in college and university. I coached and refereed hockey for years. I still play hockey today with old timers for fun, exercise and camaraderie. Hockey has defined and shaped me to be the type of person I am today.

Hockey has been intimately woven in the very fabric of the Canadian cultural identity. It can almost be compared to a religion with its unwavering adulation and devotion. The game is revered and followed by millions of people. Professional hockey players are national heroes revered and worshiped by the masses. I can remember watching a hockey game on the CBC program Hockey Night in Canada every Saturday evening. My dad would sit in his chair, along with the children spread out on the floor and we would by glued to the black and white television for close to three hours. Hockey is closely aligned to the harsh, cold Canadian climate. What else are you going to do in winter, other than chase a small disc of black vulcanized rubber around a slab of frozen ice on sharp blades of tempered steel. Hockey is fun, fast and fresh.

When I was five years old I used to go skating in our backyard on a homemade ice rink in winter. My dad would layer sheets of water and pile up banks of snow to make a tidy rink. I would dress warm and skate in the fresh cold winter air for hours on end. I used to stickhandle with a puck. I would shoot at a homemade net that we made out of two by fours and fish net mesh. The rink was dotted with small fruit trees that grew in the back yard. I would try to stick handle and dodge around the small fruit trees like I was evading a menacing foe. Some of the neighborhood friends would come over and we would engage in a heated hockey game that never seemed to end. When my mother would call me in for supper or bed I would have a big mug of hot chocolate and melted marshmallows. After inhaling the fresh winter air my cheeks were rosy, my body was exhausted and I felt sublime.

I played a lot of road hockey in my youth. We lived in a big ranch house on 17th street in Grand Forks. Down the street at the intersection of 17th and 77 avenue lived a friend named Bob. He had some old hockey nets and we played countless street hockey games there. Other neighborhood friends including Willie, Gary, Leon, Billie and Dave would gather and the fun would begin. We played for many hours at a time. We would have sticks, gloves and on old tennis ball or a hard, orange hockey ball. We tried to imitate our favourite hockey heroes. I would try to be Bobby Hull, Phil Esposito or Guy Lafleur, but my all-time favorite hockey player was Bobby Orr. Bobby Orr was the all-star defenceman for Boston Bruins. He was fast and could skate circles around all the other professional hockey players in the National Hockey League. He would score many goals and would win scoring titles. He was amazing and I tried to be like him.

On weekends in the winter time a lot of people would gather and play pond hockey. There was a pond called Saddle Lake that was located up between the crest between Sion and Hardy Mountain. The lake was relatively small and would easily freeze over in the early months of winter. I would usually get dropped off in the late morning or mid-afternoon and stay there for hours. The pond was probably as wide as two ice rinks and as long as four ice rinks. The ice would freeze over in a beautiful light blue colour. It was pretty smooth but sometimes there would bubbles and rocks and twigs sticking out. A heated game of shinny would began when enough players showed up. The goals were old nets with mesh or just a hat and glove to mark the perimeter of the goal. You could skate and stick handle just about anywhere around the pond. I would strive to improve my stickhandling and passing skills. I think my stick handling really improved there because there were no boards around the pond and I would be careful to control the puck. If you passed the puck or shot the puck at the net and you missed, the puck would go way down the ice. You would have to go retrieve it and other players would yell at you for missing. There was usually a big, bonfire at the edge of the pond where you could go to warm up. Some foolhardy guys would even drive their cars on the pond for excitement. It was a lot of fun playing pond hockey with my friends.

After developing some skating skills I joined an atom team at our local Grand Forks Minor Association. We played and practiced at the only rink in our town that is now called the Jack Goddard Arena in memory of a former mayor of the town. Like most arenas in small towns throughout Canada it was the heart and centre of many social activities and gatherings in our community. I made new friends and we got bright, new and clean jerseys and socks. We had an early morning practice when it was still dark outside once per week. Our coach put us through the paces with drills that were supposed to develop our skills. We skated and skated and skated some more. We stickhandled around imaginary players, pylons and other players. We passed the puck to each other. We shot at the boards and we shot on the goalies. We practiced our wrist, snap and later the slap shot. And then we played games. Sometimes we scrimmaged with each other. Other times we played the other atom team and other times we played out of town teams from Midway, Castlegar, Nelson and Trail. I loved hockey and would eagerly race to the rink at any time.

I played hockey all throughout my school years in Grand Forks, except for one year when I decided to ski for the winter. I went through the different ranks of hockey from atoms, peewees, bantams and midgets. I played on recreational house teams and when older I played in competitive rep teams. It kept me busy and out of trouble in the fall and winter months. I enjoyed the fraternization and socialization that came along when playing with other like-minded individuals. Some of my best friendships that I developed were with other hockey players. I still keep in contact with friends that I played hockey with from when I was seven and eight years old. Hockey was the enduring tie that binds.

There was an un-written code in hockey that was generally acknowledged by all the players. There were certain expectations that

40

needed to be met. You were supposed to show up on time to practice. You were expected to work hard and put effort at practice and games. You were supposed to pay attention and listen to your coach and elders. You were expected to behave with respect to coaches, players and all other people you would encounter. You were advised to dress appropriately, often in suit and tie when playing rep hockey at out of town and home games. You were expected to talk and communicate to everybody in a fair, honest and respectful manner. You were told not to swear or cuss, but when we were older that didn't seem to work out that well. You would treat other people as you would want to be treated yourself.

I played a lot of hockey games. Sometimes I played good other times not so good. Some games we won, some games we lost. I tried to work hard, sweat a lot and had a lot of fun. We travelled all around the West Kootenays and Okanagan. We went to hockey tournaments all over and they were generally a lot of fun. We got to see some very good hockey players, some of which went on to be professionals. One time we played a Kelowna team in peewees. They had one player on their team named Brady who skated circles around us. I never seen a player that good. When he was on the ice he always seemed to have the puck. He scored almost all the goals for their team. We got creamed that game and lost in double digits. I later heard he quit hockey and became a professional pool player. Another time in bantams we went to a tournament in Beaver Valley. There were eight teams there and there was a big banquet in the hall upstairs from the rink. Somehow we were supposed to help out there. Somebody asked me to carry the big jug of orange pop upstairs. I ended up dropping the container and spilled the orange crush all over the floor in front of everybody. I turned bright red and so embarrassed. Another time in midgets we went to a hockey tournament in Victoria. I learned there how cruel some people could be to others. We stayed in a motel there and were supposed to bunk four players to a room. A couple players were extremely rude and mean to another player. He was from a poor family and supposed lower social class and didn't have the best equipment. Other players made fun of him, teased him and said he smelled. Nobody wanted to bunk with him. Somehow I was chosen to be his roommate. He smelled a little, but I didn't mind.

I thought I was a pretty decent hockey player. I had some good all-around skills that needed some refining and modification. I wasn't the fastest, but I could skate pretty well. I had good hands and was a pretty good stick handler. I was a good passer and worked well with others. My shot was pretty strong. It wasn't the hardest, but I had a fast wrist shot. I usually played forward. I was the power centre. I played on the power play and I could kill penalties. I sometimes played defence, but I never played goal. I was sometimes the assistant captain, but not usually the captain. I was a little too shy and timid. I wasn't aggressive enough and I didn't like to body check that much. I didn't get penalized that often and I only ever got into one hockey fight in my entire career.

Sometimes I remember getting a little uptight before hockey games. I wanted to do my best and had pretty high expectations of myself. I remember we went to a hockey tournament in Castlegar when I was in Bantams. I usually scored goals but I was not playing to my full potential. My uncle Mike from Castlegar was watching the games and he also sensed my frustration. He decided that I needed to relax a bit and just play the game. He gave me a glass of wine before one game. It helped and I played my best game of the tournament. We won, I scored three goals and earned the first star of the game. Another time in midgets a team from Sweden was visiting. We sold tickets and the local arena was packed with spectators. We were all excited to play a foreign team in front of a big crowd. When the Swedish team stepped out on the ice, I was surprised at how small they were. The looked a little scared and daunted. Our team played well and we crushed our opponent. We beat them easily with a score of 10 to 2. I played good, scored four goals and earned the first star selection. It was ok, but I was easily a foot taller than the Swedish players and somehow it just didn't feel right.

When I was 17 years old I played for the Grand Forks Border Bruins. The Bruins were the local junior B hockey team that played in the Kootenay International Junior Hockey League or KIJHL. We were playing against some bigger and stronger players that were 20 years old. When I was younger I used to watch the Bruins play and run around the rink unabated with my friends. Sometimes they had really good teams and at other times they did not. They had stars like Gerry, Jack and Wayne Quiring. They were stars in the league and Gerry and Wayne used to win the scoring titles. They were heroes that minor hockey players looked up to and tried to emulate. Then there were other players who had nicknames like Dave "the killer" Cheechoo. He was a goon that got into fights with many of the players on the other teams. He was the nicest guy off the ice, but he was a psycho on the ice. Junior B hockey was stronger and faster than minor hockey. But it was also "bush league" hockey. There were a lot of intimidation and pandering and lots of unnecessary fighting. I was a little too timid and skinny at this time. There were other players who were older and better than me. I was a role player on the team. I did ok, it was fun and I grew up pretty quickly.

I am a product of the Minor Hockey System in Canada. I went through the ranks, learned their techniques and practiced their procedures. I had a lot of fun playing hockey, grew up and learned how to act and behave as a responsible adolescent and later as an adult. I had many hockey coaches and mentors throughout the years. Some were good, some were bad and a few were excellent. I had a great coach that liked me, encouraged and believed in me. Coach Mike was my favorite coach. He moved from Vancouver with his three sons to Christina Lake. He coached in bantams, midgets and the Border Bruins. He was heuristic and practical. He inspired, motivated and helped me gain confidence. He helped to actualize me as a hockey player and as a person.

When I went away to College and later University, I continued to play hockey. I played for the Selkirk Saints when I went to college in Castlegar. We were basically a bunch of pretty good hockey players that got together and scrimmaged a couple of times per week. The forestry faculty in school seemed to have the best players. They were rugged and tough. When I went away to Vancouver I attended the University of British Columbia. I usually played up to five times per week there at the Thunderbird Sports Rink. I played for different faculties including science, arts, engineers and dentistry. I tried out for the varsity hockey team in third year there. Training camp was gruelling and we would have to run outside around the endowment lands. I made the junior varsity team, but dropped out because it was was interfering with my studies. When I went to school in Seattle, Washington at Bastyr College I continued to play hockey. Unlike Vancouver, Seattle only had a few rinks. Drop in hockey was expensive. I decided to try join the University of Washington hockey team. I didn't go to the school, but I could play hockey pretty well and they needed some good players. The coach really liked me, didn't ask me too many questions and let me play for the team for several years. We played other junior B teams, and other college and university teams throughout the Pacific Northwest. I really enjoy playing for the UW team.

Uncle Mickey the Barber

Now I am older and live in Kelowna, BC. I have continued to play hockey, mainly for exercise, fun and recreation. My passion for the game has continued to coaching and even refereeing. I have coached my two girls all throughout their careers in Kelowna Minor Hockey from atoms to midgets. Now I just player hockey with a group of old timers. I never thought that this day would come. I used to be fast and strong and could score a lot of goals. Now I am not so strong and fast and I don't score as many goals as before. I seem to fit right in and I still have a lot of fun playing and enjoy the camaraderie around the game. In the words of Red Green from the Canadian classic Red Green Show, "keep your stick on the ice."

CHAPTER 6

Toil and Peaceful Life

There is an old saying that to figure out where you going, you have to know where you are coming from. In the iconic reggae song called Buffalo Soldier by Bob Marley he sings "If you know where you are coming from, then you wouldn't have to ask me, who the heck do you think I am, because you would already know." We all belong some place. We are all from someplace else. We all come for some place other than the place we are currently at. Everybody has roots, ancestry and a past. Some people want to remember their past and some people want to forget. Some people honour and respect their history and others prefer to let the past go. Others want to learn of the past history to give an inclination of what they should do for their future. Canada is a cultural mosaic of different nationalities, races and cultures. This country is made up of immigrants from all around the world. All have come here to have a better life. Unlike the American potpourri melting pot, we are encouraged to retain part of past cultural identity. I wanted to know about my ancestry, my roots and my ancestry. I wanted to know a little bit about my past to help me learn about the future.

My mother Marion was from Russian Doukhobor ancestry. Her mother's maiden name was Mary Ogloff and her father's name was Bill Kurnoff. There were first generation immigrants from Russia. They were members of the Russian Christian group called Doukhobors. They were a group of common Russian peasants who questioned the beliefs and tenets of the Russian Orthodox Church during the late 17th and 18th centuries. As a result, they were ostracized and persecuted for the beliefs. The ruling tsar of Russia banned their beliefs. He exiled members of the group to the Caucasus region, Georgia and Siberia. Then the Russian government instituted mandatory army conscription service. The Doukhobors refused to comply. Instead they gathered up all the guns and armaments, put them in a big pile and burned them. The tsar was furious. He decided that the easiest way to get rid of this meddlesome group was to allow them to immigrate somewhere else. He allowed them to leave if they promised not to come back, paid their own way and finished their prison term if they were incarcerated. About 6000 Doukhobors immigrated to Canada in 1899. They originally settled in Saskatchewan were land was given to them to farm. They then moved to British Columbia and settled in Grand Forks and Castlegar. They are now over 40,000 people of Doukhobor descent in Canada today.

Doukhobors are a Russian Christian group that believes the spirit of God is within each person. The word Doukhobor means "spirit wrestler." They were given this name because they didn't believe the mainstream Russian orthodox religion. They were restless and unsettled. They questioned the status quo religion and were believed to be wrestling with the very spirit of God itself. They had community prayer meetings called molenie. They sang Christian hymns in acapella style, often in the Russian language. They used bread, salt and water to symbolize the necessity of the basic elements to sustain life. They were hard working and formed collective farms and built factories to process and distributed food. They believe that God is an energy force that can be summed up in the one word; love. True Doukhobors are vegetarians because they reject violence against all beings. The do not partake in alcohol, smokes and other drugs. The refuse military service in that they believe it is wrong to kill another living being. Their belief can be summed up in a paraphrase of the Golden Rule. Do unto others as they would do unto you. The old Russian proverb summarizes what it means to be Christian. It says, you judge a flower by its scent, an apple by its taste and a Christian by their deeds.

My mother said Little Totya was priceless. She exemplified unconditional loving, caring and giving. Little Totya was my auntie who lived by the black train bridge on the Kettle River east of Grand Forks just past the airport. I learned that her real name was Lukeria and she was my mother's dad's sister. She was married to Kooza. She was short and less than five feet tall. She spoke very little English, but was fluent in Russian. When I was young I had trouble communicating with her because I didn't speak Russian that well. I took lessons in elementary school and high school for a few years, I could converse a little bit, but I certainly wasn't fluent. My dad didn't or couldn't speak Russian that well. He said that he forgot the language when he immigrated over to Canada when he was nine years old. My mother spoke fluent Russian but didn't speak that much around her children. She would speak in Russian when she was talking on the phone to one of her friends or relatives. She would sometimes chatter on for an hour or more when she was in a deep conversation with one of her Russian compatriots. Little Totya could say and understand some basic words and phrases in English. I used to talk in simple syllables, uttered short phrases and made it a fun game to try talk to her. We used to go visit Little Totya and Kooza.

Kooza and Lukeria lived in a small one story sharply gabled house at the edge of the river bank. They only had one bedroom in the house and only recently had water and electricity. They used to have to fetch water from a well outside. They used to have an outhouse just outside and away from their house. They used to have a wood stove to heat the house in winter. They had a big garden on their land for fresh fruits and vegetables. As far as I know they were vegetarian. The house smelled of age and old people stuff. We used to sit at the table in the kitchen. Little Totya would serve a delicious lunch of Russian food and pastries. Kooza spoke only some broken English. They didn't have a television in the house and I thought it was boring hanging out there. Sometimes we would try to play cards there sitting around the small table to keep busy. My mother told me when I was born, Little Totya asked her what she named me. My mother told her my name was Douglas. Doggie she said. She couldn't understand why my mother would name me after a dog.

Little Totya came by boat from Russia when she was a young child. She had a sharp mind, but didn't or couldn't go to school past the early elementary grades. She got married to Kooza, but wasn't able to have children for some reason. She was the older sister of my mother's dad Bill. She took care of my mother and her older brother Mike. When Marion's parents were off working picking fruit or working in a packing factory, it was Little Totya that took care of the children. I think this is why my mother always spoke highly of her and had a special fondness with her. They had a special bond.

Little Totya would work hard. When she was young she used to work at Davidoff's farm planting and doing farm work. She used to cook and can all sorts of preserves. She knitted and crocheted socks, sweaters and blankets. I remember she would make handbags and rugs out plastic bags. I think she experienced the great depression and this made her thrifty and resourceful. She would collect and recycled old plastic bags and turn them into works of art. She knitted plastic bag rugs, hand bags and slippers. At the time I didn't think much of them, but looking back I realize how incredible her crafts were.

Little Totya was very giving. She didn't have much money or much in the way of earthly possessions. Whenever she saw me she would open her purse and give my some silver coins. She was always giving something to our family even though she didn't have much. She would give our family Russian food to eat like borscht, pirahi and vareniki and a Russian berry juice called atvar. She would give hand-made socks, sweaters, hats and blankets. She would give of her time and babysit us when my mother wasn't available.

Little Totya would like to have a drink at night time. She enjoyed her drink. I suppose it helped her relax and go to bed. She used to like to have a beer on a hot day. She used to have a flask of brandy. I would see or hear her have a swig of spirits from her flask occasionally. I never saw her drink more than one drink. She never drank in front of the children.

When Kooza died, Little Totya moved to the area closer to town called Ruckle Addition. She live with one of her younger relatives. I used to go mow her lawn there occasionally. She stayed with our family for a while when she wasn't well. She liked my mother and my mother loved her. Little Totya developed stomach cancer a few years later. She wouldn't complain and would always try to smile and be positive. How are you, somebody would ask? In Russian or broken English she would always answer, "I'm fine, I'm fine.' She passed away when she was in her late 70's years of age. I will always remember her as a sweet, giving soul who embodied the meaning of love.

Jane Chernoff was my aunt and my mother's first cousin. She lived in Grand Forks. Her maiden name was Kurnoff like mothers. She married Nick Chernoff at a young age. He passed away from a heart attack before the age of 50 years. They had three children together named Debbie, Walter and Jim. She remained a widow and never remarried. She raised the three children on her own on a small widow's pension. She did a lovely job raising her three children. They all turned out well with good careers and families. Jane lived in an old, small single story house with a chimney of 68th avenue.

48

Aunt Jane was an excellent cook. She had a large garden and she grew her own fruits and vegetables. I remember eating borscht, pirahi, vareniki and delicious raspberry rhubarb tarts for desert at her place many times. She also canned and preserved many fruits and vegetables. Although she had electricity she preferred to heat her house with a wood stove. Sometimes my dad and I would bring her fire wood for her stove in the winter time. She was very crafty and she crocheted and knitted a lot. She would knit hats, scarfs, mittens and socks that she gave away to many people. I would receive many hand-knitted items from her when I was young. She also crocheted large blankets called afghans. I remember many times sitting at her kitchen table playing cards with her. We used to play a Russian card game called Durak or Crazy. It was a fun game with six cards in your hand, trumps and wild cards. You would try to get rid of all your cards as fast as you could. The last one with cards remaining in their hand was a Durak or crazy. She had a living room with a black and white television. Sometimes I would sit in her living with her and watch one of the five channels on her television. Sometimes I would talk to her about what was going in my life. She was a good listener and she would often shake her head in disbelief about some of the things I was pulling off. Jane was nice lady.

Jane was a good worker and worked hard and diligently. My mother told me she helped other people a lot. She volunteered at the Russian hall. She also said that Jane used to even volunteer to help clean and prepare deceased bodies for funerals. Jane was strong and this didn't seem to bother her. She used to walk a lot with her friends and other widowers when her legs were good. She had good morals and believed in proper things. I wasn't sure if she believed in God or not, but she seemed to have strong beliefs. She was honest and fair. She told the truth and didn't lie or fabricate things. She wasn't rude but she was outspoken. Some might say she was a little rough around the edges. She would let you know if and when she didn't agree with you.

After my grandmother Mary passed away, Jane became like a second grandmother to me and my sister. She would have us over, fed us, gave us things she knitted and crocheted. When I was older I would even have a drink with her. She had an assortment of brandy, cognac and vodka. We would have a toast about something, clang glasses together and make an onerous salutation. Jane came to our wedding in Vancouver when I got married to Natalie. Like a grandmother she was pulling and pressing my tuxedo so it fit just right and I looked good. I will always remember Jane as hardworking, honest and forthright. She was wise, frugal and practical.

Nick and Helen were an older Russian couple who were good friends of my parents. Nick worked as a labourer at the local sawmill and was also a farmer. He would ask my dad to do mechanic work on his farm equipment. Helen was affable and loquacious. She would stop by and visit my mother and sometimes wouldn't leave. She would spend many hours talking in Russian and English about everything from the weather to religion and politics and everything in between. Nick and Helen had a farm near the US border at the base of Galena Mountain in the area called Almond Gardens. They had a small house there with several large barns and fields of hay, cattle and a huge vegetable garden. They had three children, Marcie, Joe and Steve who I only vaguely knew. They were older and long gone by the time I knew Nick and Helen. Nick and Helen had an enduring and often offsetting acrimonious relationship.

I remember going to their farm when I was young with my father and sometimes my mother. Nick would get my dad to do mechanical work on his broken down farm equipment. My father was a skilled mechanic who could fix just about anything. He would work on and repair one of Nick's tractor, hay baler or other broken equipment. Sometimes Nick brought the piece of machinery that needed fixing to my dad's garage. My dad said Nick was always fair and honest and paid well and on time for the work he did.

While Nick was out working in a barn or field around the farm, Helen would be in the kitchen cooking. She always seemed to be cooking or in her greenhouse or on her garden. They were both very friendly and hospitable. There always seemed to be people of all sorts, sizes and nationalities coming and going from their household. Nick was abrupt and gruff and would almost always demand Helen cook something for their visitors. She would mostly oblige and she whipped something up quickly and efficiently. Sometimes they would get in heated arguments and the expletives would fly. I have this one image of them that I will never forget. Helen was slowly driving down the dusty country road in her old Mercury car away from the house. Nick was running after her in his rubber boots, overalls and suspenders. He was yelling and screaming about something that was oblivious and unintelligible to Helen as she was driving away.

Regardless of their marital shortcomings, they were always entertaining and welcoming.

Nick had a full stock of booze and spirits to fuel the entertainment and soothe the visitors. I think a lot of people liked going to his place because he was free and giving with his drinks. I remember there would almost always be men and women of all ages sitting around their kitchen table. It was a traditional farm house and environment. You weren't ask to take off your shoes once inside and most people didn't. There were bottles of beer and spirits cluttering the table. There was cognac, rum, vodka and other varieties of alcohol. There was always loud talking, laughing and sometimes arguing going on around at all hours of the day and night. It was a friendly, sociable and relaxed place to be.

When I was a teenager I used to work on the farm for Nick. He needed help collecting, stacking and sorting bales of hay in his fields or from some other fields. He had an old two ton truck. He would bale the hay himself. He would hire me and one or two other guys to load and transport the hay. We would load it on the truck, drive the truck to one of his barns and unload and stack it neatly inside. We were young and full of energy. The bales of hay were heavy and often weighed more than 30 or 40 kilograms (60 or 80 pounds). I needed to build muscle and this seemed to be a good way to do it. I remember reading about how the famous hockey player Bobby Hull said he used to lift and throw bales of hay on his farm in the prairies. He would do this to build muscle, power and strength in the summer to prepare for hockey. I thought this was a good idea and followed his lead. The work was hard and dirty but I enjoyed it for the most part. My friends and I would make it fun and horse around. We would do the work, but we entertained ourselves. We would often have music blaring and would see who could pile the hay the fastest. We would throw bales at each as the sweat was pouring down our faces. We often ate at Nick and Helen's house after working for him. There would also be some libations to indulge in afterwards. Sometimes Nick would insist we even have a drink before starting work. It was fun, hard work and I mostly enjoyed it.

Nick and Helen had an odd but enduring relationship. They were always entertaining and sociable. They were always friendly and hospitable to everybody and there was no distinction between different social classes of people. There always seemed to be laughter, bickering

51

and quarrelling going on simultaneously. They were always giving, magnanimous and outflowing. There seemed to be an outpouring of positive energy and good vibes at their house. Perhaps they weren't the best example of marital bliss. They had faults and character flaws, but so does everybody else. One day Helen had a stroke and passed away in her mid-sixties. Nick missed her immensely and couldn't come to terms with the loss. My parents went to console and visit him afterwards. I distinctly remember him being less sociable, cantankerous and quarrelsome than before. He would sit in his old dusty chair on the veranda porch in the front his house for hours. One day he just passed away sitting in his chair staring out over his farm and the empty fields.

I had other relatives who influenced me and helped to mentor my life. My Aunt Norma and her husband Mike lived towards downtown Grand Forks near the city park. Norma was the younger sister of my grandmother on my mother's side. Mike had diabetes and ended up losing one leg and then another to this terrible disease. They had to two grandsons named Randy and Tim from Pass Creek up the valley from Castlegar. I used to hang out and horse around with them. I used to mow Norma's lawn and do yard work for her. She was always nice and hospitable. My Aunt Lucy lived on the North Fork road out in west Grand Forks. She was my aunt through marriage to one of my mother's relatives named John Kurnoff. She was fluent in Russian and taught at the Russian community hall in our community. She was widowed at a young age and raised two children on her own. Her older daughter Lana had medical condition and she passed away in her early twenties. Lucy was very active and I remember her always walking some place. I don't think she had a car. I also had an Uncle Alex Hawerluk on my father's side. He was the only relative that I remember on my dad's side. He lived by Donaldson Park in the west end of Grand Forks in a quaint and tidy house. He was married to his wife in Anastasia. They had no children. He owned and operated a small grocery store called the West End Store for many years.

I have been fortunate to have many other relatives, friends and acquaintances who have had a positive influence on my life. I came from Russian Doukhobor and Polish background that is strongly rooted in Christian beliefs. I was exposed to this culture and their convictions by the people I met growing up in Grand Forks. I learned by example and watching and observing other people around me. I am now a third generation Canadian and I adhere to some of the faith and tenets I was

52

exposed to. In many ways I have had a privileged childhood and upbringing. I have a firm sense of my past and this has helped shape my present and future. I strongly believe in the Doukhobor Russian tenet that you should toil and have a peaceful life.

CHAPTER 7

Phoenix and the Tamaracks

Phoenix was a beautiful and accessible gateway to the back country and wilderness between Grand Forks and Greenwood. It was a four season playground and museum of the past. Phoenix represented the approximately 25 by 40 kilometre land mass between Grand Forks to the east, Greenwood to the north, Midway to the west and the Canada-United States border to the south. It was an elevated, rounded plateau interspersed with small mountains and hills. It was the southern part of the Monashee Mountain range between the Okanagan Valley desert to the west and the jagged and rugged Selkirk Mountains to the east. Geologically speaking it was pretty average and boring. It was formed from metamorphic and sedimentary rock of the late Paleozoic and Mesozoic eras. It included breccia, conglomerates and lava forms made up of granite, limestone and chalcopyrite. It was rich in foliage from trees including cottonwood, fir, larch, pine and spruce. It was abundant in wildlife including mule and white-tailed deer, black bear, bobcats, cougar, porcupine, coyote, ospreys and bald eagles. It was a venerable landscape full of life and rich in history.

To me, Phoenix meant the ghost town, the abandoned mine, the ski hill, the toboggan hill and the cross country trails near Marshall Lake. Phoenix also meant the backroads and trails just west of Grand Forks on Highway 3, as it curved its way up Spencer's Hill and out of the Sunshine Valley towards Greenwood. It encompassed the hills and mountains above July Creek as it paralleled the highway north to Loon or Wilgress Lake. It included the creeks and valleys that flowed into July Creek like Gibbs Creek, May Creek, Skeff Creek and Lind Creek. It was a place to explore a forlorn ghost town that was once a thriving mining community. It was a region to go gold panning and search for lost mines and treasure. It was an area to go hiking and mountain bike riding. It was a spot to gather firewood and go hunting for mule and white tailed deer. It was a location to go downhill alpine skiing and to go cross country skiing. It was a place to explore, have fun and imbibe the natural beauty around you.

In July 1891, two prospectors named Henry White and Matthew Hotter staked claims on a patch of knobby hills located between Grand Forks and Greenwood. They were looking for silver and gold. They aptly called their original claims appropriately Knob Hill and Old Ironsides. They found some rock and ore rich in copper. Other prospectors including Bob Denzler and George Rumberger joined the pair, staked claims and began mining in the area. George Rumberger would also go on to be the first mayor of the incorporated town of Phoenix. Soon many other prospectors joined them and there was reported to be over one hundred claims around the region. They mined the area for several years till a conglomerate of investors from eastern Canada and the United States took an interest in the property. The investors purchased several claims and formed the Granby Mining, Smelting and Power Company. A large scale mining operation was opened and the gold rush was on.

The area around the mine was originally called Greenwood camp. A town site was constructed around and literally between the mines. At this time Phoenix was considered the highest city in Canada at an elevation of 1400 metres or 4500 feet. It was located at the top of the ridge 11 kilometres east of Greenwood. From Grand Forks you would follow what would be the Crowsnest Highway 19 kilometres north and west before turning left and winding your way up the hill for another 15 kilometres. The town site was located within a short walking distance close to the actual mines. There was an upper Phoenix and a lower Phoenix separated by a ravine. Canadian Pacific or C.P. railway and Great Northern or G.N. constructed rail lines from Eholt to Phoenix and Phoenix to Grand Forks to ship ore to smelters located in Grand Forks, Greenwood and Boundary Falls. With an influx of miners, labourers and support workers, the city of Phoenix was born and was incorporated in 1898.

In the early 1900's, Phoenix was a busy active city. People flocked to the area and soon the population of Phoenix swelled to 1800 permanent residents. There were over 600 miners and the rest were support workers and children. Phoenix started with a one room school house that grew to a school with four separate classrooms. Dr. Boucher moved to the city, operated a hospital clinic and became the town's resident doctor. Judge W.R. (Willie) Williams moved to the town from

Winnipeg and became the city's first and last magistrate. He was a tall, lanky gregarious man over 6 feet 7 inches in height. He colloquially called himself the tallest judge in the highest court in Canada's highest city. Phoenix had a newspaper called the Phoenix Pioneer. It had two telegraph and telephone companies and a power and lighting company. It had a brewery, several hardware and dry goods stores and several grocery and food stores. There were several barber shops and a furniture store. Phoenix had 24 hotels and boarding houses with names like Brooklyn, Maple Leaf, Queens, Summit and Victoria. There were several restaurants and more than a few saloons. The taverns were full of tired miners who liked a drink and enjoyed card and gambling games. Phoenix had a three storied union hall complete with banquet room, opera house and dancing hall. There was also a big covered hockey rink with a beautiful arched ceiling with seating for up to a 1000 people. Their hockey team won the British Columbia Championship in 1911. There was even a female hockey team wearing skirts and skates. At the turn of the century, Phoenix was a city full of excitement and teaming with life.

During its peak operation, the mines at Phoenix were sending over one million tons of ore to the smelters in Grand Forks, Greenwood and Boundary Falls. Some miners dug by hand with shovels and picks. Others used jack hammers and other machines to drill into the earth. Mining cars and trailers steadily emerged from mining shafts loaded with rock and ore. Large, elaborate mechanical conveyor belts and processing devices moved the ore to rail cars waiting close by. The trains were busy transporting rock and ore to these smelters seven days a week. One occasions one of locomotives would jump the tracks and crash during its steep descent to the valley bottom. All told, the mines at Phoenix extracted close to 14 million tons of ore from the bowels of the earth there on that rounded, knobby hill of volcanic rock.

Everything was going along great till World War 1 broke out in Europe in 1914. The demand for copper decreased sharply and the price of the metal plummeted significantly on world markets. With decreased demand and drop in copper price, the mines at Phoenix struggled to exist. Times became tougher after the end of the war in 1918. The Granby mining company laid off miners and labourers. Stores, restaurants and saloons all lost business. People started to leave the city in droves. In June of 1919, the Granby Consolidated Mining Company ceased operations altogether and closed the mines for good. All the remaining workers and people in the town left the town once and for all. The change was so dramatic and sudden many people just left their homes and businesses and walked away taking nothing but the clothes on their back. Buildings were left empty, many restaurants were left with settings still in place and houses were left emptied with dishes still in the sink. The city of Phoenix came a quick and abrupt end by year's end.

In the 1920's the city was slowly dismantled and many of the buildings and chattels were sold off and carted away. In the 1930's many of the remaining structures were demolished and destroyed. By the 1940's not much remained of this once vibrant and busy mining community. Only a few hearty souls remained. Aldolf Sercu was a Belgium born immigrant who was known as the caretaker of what remained of Phoenix at this time. He had an arm brace fitted over one arm and was known by the nickname Forepaw. He passed away in 1942. William Brambury was known as the last mayor of Phoenix by his friends. He owned part of what remained in Phoenix and eagerly awaited for its resurgence. He passed away in 1951.

In the 1950's there was a renewed interest in the copper main after copper prices steadily increased. The newly reformed Granby Consolidated Mining Company was formed in 1955 and started mining some of the old claims called Old Ironsides and Snowshoe. This time the mining activity was an open pit mine that stripped away the earth on these claims around the old town site. They used large vehicles including bulldozers, graders and big dump trucks. A tailings pond was created just down the hill from the mine towards Greenwood. They stripped away the earth in layers exposing the dull yellow, brown earth. The mine operated until 1976, when copper prices decreased and it was no longer financially feasible to continue operation. This time there was not much of town site and no mass exodus like before. Again Phoenix was closed and another mining era came to an abrupt end. This time however, there would be no further resurgence and rebirth of this once active and vibrant city.

I used to the Phoenix Ski Hill with my class mates from Perley Elementary School on ski days in grade 5. We used to take the bus up the Phoenix road and turn sharply right just before you get to the top of the mountain. We would skirt around the side of a mountain for another 5 kilometres and then descend to the base of a mountain. There was a small, quaint community run ski hill called Phoenix Mountain. It had a tee bar that lifted skiers from the bowl at the bottoms to the top of the mountain.

Uncle Mickey the Barber

There was also a rope tow on the side for beginner skiers. I learnt to ski there on the rope tow. I held on the rope as it was moving up the gently slope to a big pulley that returned the rope down the slope and back again in continuous loop. The rope was pretty fast moving and I had to pay attention so that it wouldn't rip off your gloves and you would rope burn. After I gained confidence and became a better skier doing the snow plow and stem turns I was ready for the T-bar. The T-bar was an inverted T-shaped bar attached to a rope that was attached to the main cable overhead. A lift operator would grab the T-bar extending the upper rope and allow me to lean back and let the bottom side of the bar pull up my rear end. I held on the main part of the T-bar, bent my knees and held my ski poles with my free hand. I held on tightly and was pulled up the mountain. Many times I was paired up with another skier or went solo and did a balancing act as I heled on tightly. I moved up the slope to the first and second tower and then past the third tower where the steepness sharply increased. Beyond third tower I had to pay attention to make sure I wouldn't fall off the T-bar and slide down the mountain. Once I crested over the top of mountain I would dismount and let the T-bar go as it was retracted back to the main cable. I would do this over and over again for a full day of skiing.

At the top of the mountain I went to the left or right or turned around and went down the steep face of the mountain. To the right was the Bobcat run that had a branch off the main run called Little Annie. To the left was the flatter and more congenial Stemwinder and Lizard runs and the steeper Gypsy and Power Line runs. In all there were 16 trails and runs on the mountain. At the bottom of the mountain was a ski chalet with a change area, washrooms and a cafeteria upstairs. There was also a ski shop for rentals next door. The mountain has a vertical elevation of 215 metres (705 feet) from the base of the mountain with the elevation of the top of the mountain being 1479 metres (4652 feet) above sea level. The mountain usually got an average snowfall in excess of 8 metres (350 inches) per year.

I broke my leg on a school trip in grade 5. I was skiing down the Bobcat run just above the rope tow area. I was still learning how to ski and maneuver, but I thought I was some sort of hot dog. As I was skiing down the slope I noticed some female skiers I knew in my grade off the rope tow. I thought I would impress them and show off my skiing prowess. I decided to take a jump just off the side of the run. However, I

58

under estimated the size of the jump and flew over the bump with good velocity. I was airborne with my arms and legs struggling to gain balance and steady myself. I flew a good horizontal distance before landing awkwardly on the side of one leg and doing a face plant in the snow. I thought I was ok and went to stand up. One leg seared with pain below the kneecap. I fell down and started crying. Some other skiers stopped by to offer their assistance. The ski patrol came by, did first aid, placed my in a basket and carried me off the mountain. I was taken to the Boundary Hospital in Grand Forks, had an x-ray of my leg and confirmed that my tibia bone was broken. The doctor put on some fabric mesh over my leg and then put plaster over top and a cast was created. I stayed home a few days watching cartoons on CBC and eating cheese sandwiches. When I went back to school I maneuvered around with the help of a pair of crutches. My classmates felt sorry for me and signed my cast. After five weeks my cast was removed with a circulating saw. I was back to normal, except for a bruised pride and a bashful, demure smile afterwards.

The Phoenix Ski Hill was a magnificent and wonderful experience. The air was fresh, the snow was sublime and the people were friendly and cheerful. Many times when it was dark and dreadfully overcast in Grand Forks I would drive up the mountain and ascend above the cloud line. The sun would be shining and the sky would be bright blue and scattered with a few white clouds. I would ski with friends, socialize in the chalet and imbue the natural beauty around me.

I would also go cross country skiing at Marshall Lake at the top and to the right of Phoenix Mountain. I would drive just past the location of the old Phoenix town site, turn right and go to a little lake at the top of a crest. Marshall Lake had some cross country trails that were groomed and some trails that had no tracks. I could ski around the perimeter of the lake and then continue west slightly down sloped towards Greenwood and back again. When I was feeling especially energetic I would ski down a road to the power lines and traverse the line till meeting up with another cross country trail later. The power line trail was ungroomed and usually thick with snow. I would work hard to break trail and huff it up and down over the Hydro Line road. Except for my friend Steve, almost all the other people who we were skiing with me would complain and cuss at me for taking them off trail on this strenuous and long, ungroomed trail. The hot chocolate and other aperitifs at the end were soothing and warming enough.

Uncle Mickey the Barber

At about 8 kilometres up the Phoenix road from Highway #3 was a large pile of light coloured clay and dirt from the previous mining operation on the mountain. It made a natural slope that was perfect for tobogganing in winter time. Many local residents would climb the short distance to the flat plateau on top of the pile. At the apex you would place your toboggan on any number of paths and zoom down the mountain side. On weekends it was usually busy with children and adults having fun sliding in the snow. Sometimes at the bottom of the hill you would come to a sudden and unexpected halt to your ride. You had to be careful about some of the jumps along the way and the tree stumps at the end. Snowmobilers would be racing back and forth at the top of the hill over the plateau. Other snowmobilers would be following the old forestry roads and unused, derailed railway lines.

My dad and I used to go get fire wood just east and south of the old Phoenix town site along Number 7 or Lone Star Road. The Phoenix region was rich in trees like Aspen, Birch, Cottonwood, Douglas Fir, Engelmann Spruce, Larch or Tamarack and Lodgepole and Ponderosa Pine. My dad told me Larch was a very good burning tree for firewood and so we sought out seasoned Larch trees. We would load up his old GMC truck on weekend mornings and head up the mountain. We would have axes, chainsaws and picks to help fall the trees. Once fallen we would chop the trees in smaller, approximate 30 centimetre or one foot sections for easier splitting and transport. We would work like beavers and fill the back truck box with wood. My dad put up side rails on the box of the truck to allow us to overfill the back. We would get slightly more than one cord of wood per load. We would have lunch and a hot coffee at mid-day from our thermos, work a little more, then return down the mountain back home. The air was usually fresh and pungent from the oils and other organic compounds emitted by the abundant green trees. After the hard work you would feel pleasantly euphoric for the rest of the day and well into the evening.

The autumn months and the fall season is my favorite time of year. The days are warm, but not too hot and the evenings are cool and comfortable. Going up the Phoenix Road in fall is spectacular and stunning. Herbs and plants like Arrow-leaf Balsam root, Fireweed, Indian Paintbrush and Lupine are scattered along the sides of the road and the logging clear cut areas. They have finished their summer bloom, losing their colours and changing with the season. Light honey coloured patches of dry grass are waving gently and rustling softly in the wind. The abundant deciduous conifer trees including Aspen, Cottonwood and Larch are turning the colours of apricot orange, copper brown and lemon yellow. The bright palette of fall colours is a pleasant stimulation to my optic nerve. The whole fall spectacle is soothing to my soul.

All that remains of old Phoenix town site is a flattened chunk of earth and gravel between the saddle of a few mountains. There are no industrial buildings, houses, hotels and no other vestiges of the past. There is no sound of miners clanking their tools against the rocks of the mines, no sound of an approaching train and no sound of laughter and life that was once here. There is only the sound of silence and the wind sweeping through the trees and a few birds chirping in the distance. The openings to the old mine shafts have been blasted and filled up leaving the appearance of termites on log. The sides of the mountains have been carved and layered in terraces due to open pit strip mining. The exposed rocks and earth are rough and drably coloured in pale browns and dark yellows. Down the road towards Greenwood is a yellow and green coloured tailings pond with a clay and dirt berm. Further down the road is the quiet and overgrown Phoenix cemetery. The only remaining reminder of this once glorious city is a slender granite cenotaph with the names of those Phoenix residents who fought and died in World War 1.

The Phoenix was a colourful and vibrant bird in Greek mythology that died in flames and fire then rose from the ashes back to life again. The Phoenix symbolized rebirth, regeneration and renewal. The turn of the century mining city of Phoenix lived, prospered and died and had a short period of regeneration and renewal. However, its rebirth was short-lived and unlike the Phoenix bird, did not rise again back to life. For some Phoenix is now nothing more than a bare ghost town and memory of the past. For others it is a place full of fun and adventure including a skiing, hiking, bicycling, snowmobiling, hunting, wood cutting or just a place to enjoy the incredible beauty of nature.

CHAPTER 8

Faron My Huckleberry Friend

I read the classic book "The Adventures of Tom Sawyer" by Mark Twain when I was twelve years old. The story is about the misadventures of a young Tom Sawyer and his best friend Huckleberry Finn, as they grew up on the banks of the Mississippi River. Tom Sawyer was the clever, but sometimes lazy and misguided youth that frequently got into trouble when he hung out with his friend Huckleberry Finn. Huckleberry Finn was the affable, but meddlesome youth that frequently got into precarious situations. He was carefree, wild and some would say he was a hooligan. He frequently skipped school and didn't do homework and then dropped out altogether. He went barefoot in the summer, wore overalls and a straw hat and smoked a corn cob pipe. He liked to go fishing and hunting and lived outdoors. He lived a carefree life and didn't really fit in regular society. He was motherless and had a poor relationship with his father. He was poor and he stole watermelons and chickens to eat. He was the juvenile pariah of the town where he lived. Mother's described him as idle, lawless, vulgar and just plain bad. They cordially hated and dreaded him. Huckleberry Finn liked to smoke and swear a lot. Tom and Huckleberry had an odd but enduring friendship. Tom liked Huck a lot because he was enamoured by Huck's freedom and ability to do whatever he wanted. Huckleberry had trouble fitting in society and adopting its norms, but he had a good heart. Looking back on my youth and growing up in Grand Forks, I had a friend that closely reminded me of Huckleberry Finn.

I first met Faron in grade 5 when I was twelve years old at the Perley Elementary School in Grand Forks. I heard a new kid moved to town from Vancouver. He was gangly and wiry with wavy dirty blond hair. He liked recess and sports more than he liked school. He used to get into trouble because he was talking and not listening. He liked to socialize and have fun more than he liked listening to teachers. He liked girls and used to talk them up when most of boys would avoid them and not play with them. He was a fast runner and moved like the wind on a stormy day. He did really well on the sports days at school and won most of the first place ribbons. I liked him because he was carefree, wild and entertaining.

I got to know Faron when he joined our peewee hockey team at the Grand Forks Minor Hockey Association. He couldn't skate very well and he decided to be a goalie. He told me he learned to play lacrosse when he lived in Vancouver. He said the lacrosse helped be a goalie in hockey. At first he was awkward on his skates, but with practice and determined effort he became better. His balance was a bit off, but he tried hard and he had fast reflexes. Our team played in Midway, Castlegar, Nelson and Trail. We went to tournaments. We got better and did okay. We won some games and we lost some games. We all loved hockey and we had a lot of fun.

In grade 8 we moved across the street from elementary school to GFSS or Grand Forks Secondary School. We were mixed with older kids all the way to grade 12. It was 1978 and I was shy and uncomfortable. I liked to read, wore preppy sweaters and did really well at my classes in school. I was kind of nerdy and started to wear glasses because I couldn't see the blackboard clearly. Faron continued with his general disdain of academic school work. He really liked physical education and shop classes like drafting, woodwork and metal work. He asked me to tutor him in some of his academic courses. I encouraged him to read to improve in English skills. I gave him some of my favorite books to read including Encyclopedia Brown, The Mad Scientist's Club and The Hitchhiker's Guide to the Galaxy. One time I remember how excited he was because he read a book I persuaded him to read called The Outsiders. The book was about the misadventures of a rebellious youth named Poneyboy. He really enjoyed it and did well on the English test that followed. We were kind of an odd couple, but we had a good friendship.

I used to go visit Faron at his family's house that was located east of Grand Forks just before the rural area known as Gilpin. Their place was located just across the Atwood Bridge as it crossed the Kettle River at the base of Galena Mountain. They had a small hobby farm of a few acres. There was an old house, a garden, a rustic red barn and a fenced area with chickens and a horse. We had a lot a fun playing around the farm and exploring the areas up and down the road and along the Kettle River.

Uncle Mickey the Barber

Faron had an older brother named Dean. He didn't really like as much as he tolerated us. I thought he was really cool and he reminded me of Fonzie from the 1970's sitcom Happy Days. He wore jeans, a white t-shirt and a leather jacket with his dark wavy hair slicked back. He drove an old Jeep truck and had a girlfriend. He was popular and went to parties. Faron liked to pull pranks. I remember once his grandfather came to visit and stayed at their Gilpin home. He was old and fell asleep on a chair in the basement. As he was snoring away Faron carefully put a glass of water on his lap. When he woke up the water fell on his lap and wet his pants.

One time when his parents were away we took his family's big old tractor for a joy ride. We were under age and had no licence, but it felt like fun and a good idea at the time. It was Friday evening and we decided to drive the tractor to his friend Lane's place which was a couple of miles down the road in Nursery. We grabbed some wine from his parent's cooler and started up the tractor. Faron sat in the driver's seat and I hung on the back as we lumbered down the road at low speed. He deftly maneuvered the large behemoth as the engine revved away and we lumbered down the road. I forever have the image of Faron driving the tractor down that country road. He wore jean overalls and a bent straw cowboy hat. His hands were gyrating back and forth as he was maneuvering the large steering wheel. We drove up and down several country roads laughing and looking for girls between the farms and empty fields of hay. We got a few curious stares by other vehicles with older drivers that wondered what we were up to. We finally made it out to Lane's place. He thought we were crazy, but he came with us to take the tractor back home. We never did get into trouble and Faron's parents never did find out that we took the tractor out. We sure did have a lot of fun that evening.

I joined the track and field team in high school. I remember diligently practicing after school for discus, javelin, high jump and sprinting events. Faron was already on the track team and was a naturally gifted athlete. He was fast and had powerful legs. He excelled at the 100 metre sprint and the hurdles. We used to travel by school bus to track and field meets in Warfield just on the bench between Trail and Rossland. We used to complete in all the events in either the pentathlon or decathlon. Faron usually came in first or second in most events. He almost always won the 100 metre hurdles and other running events. I tried hard, lumbered away and finished somewhere in the middle of the pack in most of the events. Faron also liked to play other sports including basketball, soccer, volleyball and rugby in school. We took tae kwon do martial art classes together after school. He was very flexible and he could easily do the splits. He liked the sparring and we punched and kicked each other in heated revelry many times. I had a lot of bruises from his front and round house kicks. We also spent time in the gym lifting weights to strengthen our upper and lower body. I was bigger than him, but he was pretty strong for his size. Faron loved sports and competing more than he liked school.

Faron loved being around water and the Kettle River. His family moved to a Spanish hacienda house right next to the Kettle River just past the airport outside the city limits just east of Grand Forks. They converted the garage into a bedroom for him. He used to have pet pigeons there in cages that he liked to set free and fly away. There was a big slab of concrete in their back yard right in front of the river as it ebbed by. He had man parties and barbecues there overlooking the beauty and tranquility of the river. We used to go exploring and fishing all along the river. We went canoeing, tubing and rafting up and down the river. A short distance away from his house was a black steel train bridge that crossed over the river. We spent a lot of time there swimming and jumping off the bridge in summer time. The Kettle River had a special allure and attraction for Faron.

Faron was a charmer and a lady's man. He liked girls and had a special way with them. He was suave and good looking. He could talk to girls and they liked him. I had difficulty connecting with them one some level. I was awkward and socially inept in some ways. They were different and exotic. Over the years Faron had many girlfriends. He would see a pretty girl and he would want to date her and she would want to go out with him. He treated his girlfriends nice. He took them to movies at the theatre. He bought them milkshakes, french fries, bracelets and flowers. He liked to go dancing at school dances. I would tag along with him and be his sidekick. We would go knocking on many doors to visit girls throughout the valley. He who would confide in me about many of his romantic escapades. I remember once when we were about 15 years old, an older Miss Grand Forks beauty queen took a liking to him and they had a fling after one of the parties at his house. He told me all about it. Another time we went to City Park with a pair of girls. He liked the pretty one and we were playing truth or dare games near the swings and sand box. On a whim the other girl kissed me on the cheek after a dare .and I was ecstatic for a week afterwards. Faron taught me how to socialize, meet girls and talk to them.

One time when I was 16 years old we went to the Peachfest in Penticton. Faron heard that there was a pretty girl named Arlene there who was the cousin of a friend from Grand Forks. He wanted to meet her and we hitched a ride with somebody to Penticton. We got dropped off and went to the park near the south end of Okanagan Lake. A midway and circus was set up full of rides and games. Faron met Arlene who had long blond hair and nice figure. I got stuck with her not so glamorous friend as we wandered through the carnival. We played games and tried to win the ladies stuffed animals and other prizes. We ate hot dogs, french fries and cotton candy. We went on rides including the ferris wheel, octopus and the tilt-a-whirl. It was after one of the rides that spun us around at high velocity that my date threw up all over me. I was not impressed, but Faron said he had one the best times there.

In grade 11 and 12 in high school I focused on academic course like biology, physics, chemistry and math. I wanted to go to college and university afterwards and maybe become a doctor or scientist. I saw less of Faron as he took more industrial and shop courses. I was still playing hockey at this time and Faron had dropped out several years earlier. He still liked to have fun and party. I saw him at outdoor parties at places like the motor cross and the Pits up North Fork on Friday and Saturday nights. He also had a steady girlfriend and he spent more time cruising around with her. By this time he had a car. He had a hot and impressive Pontiac Trans Am muscle car. I remember in grade 12 in his exuberance to celebrate high school graduation he decided to paint a large "Grad 83" on the side of Observation Mountain. He painted large letters near to top of the mountain overlooking Grand Forks so that everybody could see. However, he painted the 3 of the year backwards. Faron didn't want the good times to end.

After high school graduation I went to Selkirk College and then to the University of British Columbia. I saw less of Faron and he got a job diamond drilling up in northern British Columbia. We still got together after my school was finished and I was working in Grand Forks in late spring and summer. On father's day in the middle of June of the year the Grand Forks Lions Club sponsored a big raft race on the Kettle River. The raft race would end at City Park and then there was a big celebration afterwards. Faron and I went in the raft race for several years. We were both young, strong and powerful and had a lot of fun paddling as fast as we could down the river. The first time we came in second place and the next time we won the race. Unfortunately, we had too good a time afterwards and ended up in a car crash with his Trans Am. I had some scrapes and bruises, but Faron also had a concussion. We both recovered, but seemingly went on different paths in life afterwards.

As the years went by Faron still wanted to have fun, party and socialize like we did in high school. I was in university studying and trying to get an academic vocation. He used to show up at my parent's place in Grand Forks and visit. If I was home at the time he would want to go out to a party and have a "hoedown" as he would call it. If nobody was home at our house we would often find a single flower in a little vase or empty beer bottle in the middle of our drive way for my mom or sister. I discovered that he also did this at other people's place including his former girlfriends, like Theresa and Lynne. It was special, unique and touching gesture and we knew it was only Faron who did this. It was his special calling card and reminder that he had stopped by to visit.

After I finished school I moved to Kelowna to set up my practice. I was married, had a job and two young children. I heard that Faron had got a job in Port Moody at a lumber mill. I was busy with work, life and family and we didn't talk that often. He would sometimes phone to chat and see how things were going in life and reminisce about the past. For some reason he didn't have a home or cell phone and he would phone me from work. I remember getting calls at my office from Faron when was working at the sawmill. I could barely hear him because the saws and other machinery were making so much noise in the background. He told me he lived on the outskirts of town in the country and had several large Emu animals. When my girls were still young he phoned to say he wanted to send them a large emu egg as a present. It was a nice gesture, but he failed to tell me he sent it cash on delivery in the mail. Faron seemed to have trouble giving up the past and moving forward with the reality and responsibilities of adulthood.

Faron never did get married and didn't have any children. He had a girlfriend named Vicki from New Westminster for several years, but that didn't work out. After the car accident he still had some troubles. He worked at the coast for a while and then he retired and went on disability.

Uncle Mickey the Barber

He moved back to Grand Forks and lived in a trailer on a friend's land at Christina Lake. The last time I talked to him he phoned me at my office to say he had met an Asian girl from Thailand and was going to visit her there in winter time. He asked me about malaria and what he should do to prevent it. I gave him some advice and wished him good luck. I didn't hear from him again. I learned on facebook that he had passed away in Thailand from some illness.

I am reminded of my relationship with my Huckleberry friend, Faron, by the first verse of the iconic song "Seasons in the Sun" by the Canadian singer Terry Jacks. "Goodbye to you, my trusted friend, we've known each other since we were nine or ten, together we've climbed hills and trees, learned of love and abc's, skinned our hearts and skinned our knees, goodbye to you, my friend, it's hard to die." Faron Dale Lindenbach (Moret) passed away on January 11, 2013 at the age 47.

CHAPTER 9

Volcanic Brown and the North Fork Valley

When I was a teenager in the late 1970's and early 1980's, the North Fork Valley just north of Grand Forks was my gateway to the wilderness and playground for the outdoors. I spent many hours roaming its backroads, hiking its trails and exploring the Granby River and its tributaries. I learned about its rich and colourful history and I learned a lot about myself.

Up the North Fork valley just past Ten Mile or Hummingbird Bridge was a short, steep mountain on the east side of Granby River. It flanked the right side of the road as it went north. The mountain had a distinctive large patch of dark red or rusty earth on its side clearly visible before Ten Mile Bridge. The mountain was called Volcanic Mountain. I wondered why the mountain was called this. I thought this was because the dirt resembled the colour of lava or perhaps the mountain was an extinct volcano.

I learned that the mountain was named after a turn of the century pioneer and prospector named Robert Allen Brown. I discovered that Robert Brown was one of the most colourful and quirky characters to live in Grand Forks and grace the landscape of the Boundary Country. Brown was known as Volcanic Brown and a host of other nicknames including Sunset, Golden-tooth and Crazy Brown. He was an outspoken and flamboyant miner, investor, speculator, promoter and inventor.

Volcanic Brown was slim, 5 foot 7 inches in height, had a short crewcut haircut and wore small round glasses. He usually dressed smartly with a large, wide brimmed hat, overcoat and vest and slacks and he wore heavy shoes. He was often frank and forthright. When he was in Vancouver working for CPR Railway he organized a strike for better wages. He often made his own potions and medical cures from herbs and plants he found in the wild. He used to promote and sell one magical elixir made from Oregon grape root that was supposed to cure just about everything. He once married a lady named Mary Mader for a short time and later divorced. He was arrested for shooting a killing a man who also shared the same last name as Brown. The other Brown was reportedly breaking in Volcanic Brown's cabin at the foot of Volcanic Mountain. He was acquitted of the charges as it was deemed he acted in self-defence and he was the only remaining witness of the incident. Volcanic Brown was an atheist and when in court would only say I affirm when asked to swear an oath on the bible. He prospected in the Similkameen and discovered a rich copper and gold mine there. In 1890, he sold the rights of the Sunset Mine on Copper Mountain in the Similkameen for $45,000, which at that time was a considerable sum of money.

Brown was probably born in 1849 or 1850, although the exact place and date of his birth is unknown. He first reached Grand Forks on February 22, 1884. He quickly made his way up the North Fork Valley and he set his sight on the mountain that later was called Volcanic Mountain. His preliminary mining assay showed that the mountain rock was rich in copper and gold. He staked a claim on the mountain and set up a mining operation. He sought out investors for his project and began to promote his claims. He said this site would be the richest copper mine in the country. He further elaborated that all the pencils in the world would be made from ore from this mine. He proclaimed that up to twelve railroads from the north, south, east and west would intersect at the site of Volcanic Mountain. He predicted a large city called Volcanic City would be built around the mine. His flamboyant claims were noticed by some geologists would wanted to investigate the site. These scientists determined that the mountain and ore was of low quality and was essentially worthless. Brown was upset and sued their mining company. He lost his case in court and also lost a large sum of money, over $50,000.

After this debacle Brown left the Boundary Country to investigate prospecting and mining opportunities in the Fraser Valley. He started to search for Slumach's lost placer gold mine in 1903. Legend told that an Indian fellow named John Slumach discovered a rich placer mine just beyond the headwaters of Pitt Lake. Brown would venture the region north of Pitt Lake in the summer starting in 1923. He would be gone till early autumn and he would return to civilization before first snow fall. In

1930, he went out in summer as usual, but failed to return in the autumn. A party was organized to search for him in November of that year. They found Brown's camp, his tent and supplies and even some gold nuggets he had there. However, they failed to find Volcanic Brown. He was never heard of or seen alive again.

The North Fork Road goes north from Grand Forks and curls around the west flank of Observation Mountain. The North Fork Valley opens up. It extends up past 28 Mile Bridge where the Granby River converges with Burrell Creek. The Granby River meanders through the valley flowing south to Grand Forks where it joins the Kettle River. Rich alluvial soil and gravel lines the valley bottom adjacent to the river. Pastoral farms with grass, hay and cattle dot the landscape. It is beautiful, wild and peaceful there and many times coyotes can be heard yelping in the distance in the early evening.

Snake Hole was the sandiest beach I could find anywhere along the Kettle or Granby Rivers. It was just at the beginning of the North Fork Valley where the Granby River borders the northern part of the Observation Mountain. The water was incredibly clean and refreshing. The river made a large sand bar that tickled your feet and became incredibly hot in the summer. There was a dusty dirt road branching from the North Fork Road where we would park our old truck. We would follow a short path to a rocky outcrop on the south bank of the river. Occasionally we would encounter a snake there. Sometimes it was a rattlesnake. I guess that's how Snake Hole got its name.

The old North Fork Road diverges west from the North Fork Road just past Goat Mountain. The road moves away from the Granby River around a few small mountains for about six kilometres. It meets up with the North Fork Road just over ten and a half kilometres near the old town site of Niagara. There are a few small farms and homesteads along the gravel road. This road is an excellent road to hike. I used to go for refreshing walks with my brother and sister along the old North Fork Road.

The Pines Bible Camp was located about nine kilometres up the North Fork Road on the bluffs just west of the Granby River. I remember in grade 5 spending one week at the Pines Camp in June of that year with all the other grade 5 students from Perley Elementary school. It was the first time that I was away from my home and parents for an extended period of time. There were thinly insulated cabins were we slept and a main lodge that fed us. I tried mountain climbing, bounced on a trampoline, made useful outdoor crafts, sang a lot and played a lot of games there. It was a lot of fun there.

The Pits, as it was known in our vernacular, was the site of many adolescent parties on Friday and Saturday nights. It was an old abandoned Highways gravel pit located up the North Fork Road at its junction with the old North Fork Road. I remember there was always a big bonfire burning in the middle of the gravel pit. Cars and trucks would park around the gravel pit. Someone would have late 1970's and early 1980's music blaring in the night. Rock bands like Loverboy, Trooper and Van Halen would echo across the pit. People would stand around the bonfire listening to music and drinking beverages. Teenage boys would co-mingle with teenage girls. There would be a lot of laughter infused with uncomfortable adolescent socialization.

Fisherman Road followed Fisherman Creek slightly north and west of Niagara up between the sides of two mountains. When I was a teenager I had on old Honda 250 cc motorcycle that I used to ride and explore the North Fork Valley. I didn't have a driver's licence yet, but I would make my way up the valley to explore old, unregulated Forestry roads. I would follow the Fisherman Creek Road over the Mountain to the ghost town of Eholt near Highway 33 towards Greenwood. Along the road at the crest of a mountain I had an expansive view of the beautiful North Fork Valley. Sometimes I would go further north from Eholt and take a back road to Jewel Lake.

Hummingbird Bridge was located at approximately fifteen kilometres up the North Fork road just south of Volcanic Mountain. It crossed over the Granby River and intersected with the Granby Road as it further extended north up the east side of the river to 28 Mile Bridge. The Granby Road began in Grand Forks up the east side of the North Fork Valley. Together the North Fork Road and Granby Road made a rough thirty kilometre loop from Grand Forks that was perfect for bicycling. The road was generally flat and well paved and had a few minor hills. I bicycled around the North Fork loop countless times, many times by myself and other times with friends including girlfriends.

Snowball Creek was along Granby Road at approximately nine kilometres up from Grand Forks on the east side of the North Fork Valley. There was an operational Highway's gravel pit near Snowball Creek. This site was also used for adolescent parties. There would be a big, inviting bonfire illuminating the darkness. Loud rock music of ACDC, Bachman Turner Overdrive and Meat Loaf would echo across the gravel pit. There would be a large group of socializing teenage boys and girls. This party site was known in the vernacular as the Pits dump side, since it was north of the Grand Forks Garbage Dump.

Brown Creek Road branched off the North Fork Road just before Hummingbird Bridge on the west side of the North Fork Valley. It extended up another twelve kilometres before it crossed over and met the North Fork Road again. On some Sundays my family used to drive up Brown Creek Road in our old truck to get home made cheese from the Tesolins. The children would sit in the back of the pickup with our dog and the wind in our faces as we lumbered our way north to their farm. The cheese was white and rubbery in large circular portions the size of an ice cream pale. We would shave pieces off of the main block and quickly eat them on the way home. It was a real treat.

Pass Creek was to the west of the old Brown Creek School and the old McDonald farm. Many times my dad and I would go in his old truck along the Pass Creek Road. Sometimes we would go for firewood. The hard work of sawing and chopping wood in the fresh mountain air made me feel euphoric. Occasionally I would scout for deer along the road for my dad. Other times we would turn north to go the Rock Candy Mine. The road traverses along the creek as lush cedar and larch trees line the way. It was especially green and verdant in spring and colourful gold and yellow in autumn. A few kilometres up the Pass Creek Road you turn north and traverse the side of a mountain. You then follow a plateau for a while before descending slightly into another valley that is the site of Rock Candy Mine. There were a few holes in the side of a hill with outcrops of white, green and purplish rocks and crystals. The crystals were mainly fluorite although you could find a mixture of barite, calcite and quartz there too. Searching for crystal at Rock Candy Mine was like being on a treasure hunt.

Lynch Creek was about twelve kilometres north of Ten Mile Bridge on the east side of the North Fork Road. The road was relatively flat, smooth and paved. When I was energetic I used to cycle beyond Hummingbird Bridge and go up to Lynch Creek and back. After being in university in Vancouver I would return home in summer to work. I purchased a pair of roller blades while at school. I used to go roller blading from Hummingbird Bridge to Lynch Creek. It was fun, fast and good training for hockey and skating in the winter. I used to get some interesting looks as I was rollerblading along that stretch of road near Lynch Creek.

Xenia Lake was a small, fresh lake set atop a few mountains separating the North Fork Valley from Christina Lake to the east. At about six kilometres up from Hummingbird Bridge you take a sharp right east. You follow Miller Creek Road up to the edge of Gladestone Provincial Park. The road traverses the creek before turning sharply up the mountain side. Along the creek was plenty of cedar and hemlock. There were also plenty of berries growing along the moist terrain. We would often stop and go huckleberry picking somewhere along the road before turning up the mountain. A four wheel drive vehicle was usually preferred for travel as the road is often steep, bumpy and littered with rocks. We would go fishing in this lake. We occasionally caught some small rainbow trout. There were usually a lot of horse flies and mosquitoes up there at the lake to keep you company.

Just north of the Xenia Lake turnoff but before Lynch Creek was a long, flat straight stretch along the North Fork Road. It was over a kilometre long and was the perfect place to have drag races. Once or twice a year before the cops found out there would be night time car races. Hundreds of adolescent spectators would crowd the starting line at north end of the road. There would be an array of souped-up cars and trucks. Many engines would be revving up with no mufflers on. Music would be blaring and wheels would be squealing. Somebody would be in the middle of the road with a flag to start the cars. Other times there would be a lighting system with red, orange and yellow lights to start the race. It was all the excitement of a Jimmy Dean drag race like the movie "Rebel Without a Cause." The races would extend all throughout the night or until the police broke up the party. I remember returning back home to Grand Forks many times early in the morning with the sun rising over the eastern horizon.

The North Fork Road extends north beyond Lynch Creek for another 15 kilometres to 28 Mile Bridge where the Granby River joins
74

Burrell Creek. There were a few remote farms along the road. The pavement runs out well before the bridge. The location around 28 Mile Bridge was good for camping and fishing. I remember when I was 14 years old, a group of four friends and I went camping around there. My dad dropped us with a tent, food and supplies. We didn't have a GPS, cell phones or the internet. We were wild, free and had carte blanche to do what we wanted for a few days. We set up camp, lit a fire, went hunting and fishing and played wild, outrageous games like hide and seek in the pitch black of night. We behaved liked the boys of William Golding's book "Lord of the Flies." We had a lot of fun and returned to civilization a few days later.

When I was teenager, the North Fork Valley offered me time and space for unhindered exploration. Whether it was swimming at Snake Hole on the Granby River, motorcycling over to the ghost town of Eholt, bicycling the North Fork loop with a girlfriend, going up Pass Creek for firewood or searching for crystals at the Rock Candy Mine, watching the drag races at Lynch Creek, fishing at Xenia Lake, camping at 28 Mile Bridge or investigating the red earth of Volcanic Mountain, it was a time of freedom and independence. It was a time of exploration and discovery. It was a time of learning and growing. It was some of the best years of my life.

CHAPTER 10

Loresa, Tanya and Maggie from Hardy Mountain

Adolescent rites of passage marks a time in life between childhood and adulthood. It is a time of learning, exploring and experimenting. It is a period marked by growing pains, incongruent bonding and awkward socialization. It is time of leaving the love and safety of the parental haven and searching for nourishment elsewhere. Teenage rituals ceremoniously obfuscate the pathway to maturity.

When I was 13 years old I began to have an interest in the opposite sex. I was a shy, skinny and gangly kid. I read a lot of books and really liked learning in school. I paid attention to my teachers and focused on doing my homework. I did really well at my school work and some girls asked me to help them with homework. I played hockey, but was told I was too timid and meek. My coach's encouraged me to be more aggressive and body check more. I hung around with a group of guys that were average in school, good at sports and a little dazed around girls. I think I was a little too cerebral and a little socially uncomfortable.

Loresa was my childhood friend and first girlfriend. My first recollection of her was in grade 5 at Perley School. It was the first time I went to a school dance. The gymnasium was decorated with balloons, posters and streamers. The lights were turned off and there was a strobe light flashing. Music from the 1970's blared through some speakers set on stage. All the boys stood on one side of the gym and all the girls on the other. Boys were dressed in nice suit and ties and had short haircuts. Girls wore pretty dresses and had bows and burettes in their hair. Teachers stood idly by and encouraged the girls and boys to mingle and start dancing. At first nobody would dance, but then one or two brave boys approached the girl's side of the gym and asked somebody there to dance. Then some more boys went over and even some girls came over to ask some boys to dance.

Loresa, Tamara and Michelle from Hardy Mountain

I danced with Loresa several times that night. She had shoulder length blond hair and a nice smile. At the end of the night there was a waltz and I had the last dance with her. I walked her home from the dance that night. It was a beautiful, warm starry night and the moon was out. We walked and talked about school and life. When we got to Donaldson Park we stopped and I looked into her eyes. I thanked her for dancing with me and mumbled some other things. I asked her if I could kiss her good night. She said yes and we embraced and I gave her a little kiss. I said good night and we each turned and went our separate ways. I couldn't believe it. I kissed a girl. I was ecstatic and I was on top of the world. I skipped home to the melodic harmony of crickets and frogs and the fragrant aroma of lilacs. It was the best night of my life.

Loresa and I were more friends than we were romantically involved. She was fun and she liked to do things. She was a tomboy. She was strong and fast. She liked to play sports and she was really good at them all. She was a naturally gifted athlete. She was pretty smart in school. She had a quirky sense of humor and she was wild and free spirited. She played basketball, volleyball and tennis. She was on the track and field team in high school. I joined the track and field team and spent time practicing with her. She was good at all the events including running, high jump, discus and javelin. She loved the outdoors and I shared her passion. We spent many times together biking, hiking and swimming around the valley. We used to go hiking on Hardy and Observation Mountains looking for crystals and lost treasure. We went swimming, tubing and canoeing down the Granby and Kettle rivers. When I first got my driver's licence I used to borrow my dad's truck and load up my home made cedar strip canoe that I made in woodworking class. Loresa and I would spend many times lazily floating down and exploring the river. We went bicycling around the North Fork loop and to the general store at Danville, Washington. Loresa was also good friends with my younger sister. They used to play softball together on the same team. I used to ride my bicycle to the ball diamond and watch the girls practice and play games. Loresa's mom used to work at Ike's Café in west Grand Forks. We used to go there for pie and ice cream and sodas. Loresa and I shared a lot in common. We became good friends and hung out together.

I remember asking Loresa to skip out of school one afternoon and take a ride to Rock Candy Mine up the North Fork from Grand Forks. We were now in high school and I was probably 15 or 16 years old at the time.

Uncle Mickey the Barber

We were both busy with school and other activities and we were meeting and spending time with other people. I still liked her a lot and enjoyed spending time with her. I wanted to ask her if she would go out with me and we could be girlfriend and boyfriend. I thought taking a trip to Rock Candy Mine would allow me the time and place to talk with her about my proposition. Rock Candy Mine was located way up the North Fork up Pass Creek. It was a magical place where there were green and purple crystals of barite, calcite, quartz and fluorite.

My dad had bought me an old Honda 250 CC XL motorcycle with a grey gas tank from BF Sales. I didn't have a licence at this time, but I spent a lot of time with my motor bike. I used to love to cruise and explore the forestry and logging roads around the valley and especially up the North Fork. It was my freedom to explore the hills and mountains all around Grand Forks. So one afternoon Loresa and I skipped out of school and went to Rock Candy Mine. She sat behind me holding on my waist as we lugged our way on my motor bike to the remote mine. When we got there we set out exploring and looking for crystals in the open pits and outcrops of rock that made up the mine. When I developed enough nerve, I decided to ask her if she liked me and if there was any possibility of being girlfriend and boyfriend. She said she liked me, but only as friend. She thought I was fun but a little nerdy and boring. I smiled and said ok. I was secretly devastated and then I realized we would never be romantically aligned. After searching the mine for more crystals we got on my motor bike and headed back to Grand Forks. Perhaps I was a little upset, but I ended crashing my bike when I went a little too fast and wide around a corner. My front wheel caught some loose gravel and down we went. Fortunately we did not get injured except for some bent handle bars and a bruised ego. We laughed and then continued on our way home.

Afterwards, we remained somewhat distant friends and grew apart when we went separate ways after high school. I went to Selkirk College and then to University of British Columbia in Vancouver. Loresa went to Western Washington University and studied sports management. She later moved to Halifax, Nova Scotia and worked for a hotel in hospitality and tourism management. She developed a keen interest in painting and art. She liked to travel and made several trips to Jamaica. I used to talk to her once in a while when we crossed paths in Grand Forks. She didn't use social media a lot but the last time I communicated with her was when she sent me an email. She said she was still in Halifax working and doing

Loresa, Tamara and Michelle from Hardy Mountain

artwork and was doing a detoxification cleanse. She was fatally hit by a big truck while biking to work in the morning of October 7, 2015.

From the front window of our family home on 17th street there was a beautiful view of Hardy Mountain to the west. The mountain is generally flat and boring and covered with trees, all except for a bare steep sided ridge in the middle. The ridge contrasts the rest of the mountain and is usually covered in honey coloured grass and is littered with some rocky outcrops. At the top of the ridge near the top of the mountain is a house and collection of other buildings. At night time you can especially notice the house because of the light twinkling from the mountain down the valley. The house and the surrounding buildings were known as the Hardy Mountain School. Nobody knew much about the school or the people that lived up there. Some said the school was an alternative school catering to juvenile delinquents. Others said the school has a hippy school catering to anti-establishment draft dodgers. I asked around and learned that Anne and Waldo Dahl started the school to help students who had difficulty in the regular school system. Both were teachers and wanted to establish a Waldorf type school in Grand Forks. Either way it was mysterious and intriguing.

I decided to explore around Hardy Mountain. I had a grey coloured Honda 250 cc motor bike that my dad had bought for me when I was fourteen years old. My motorcycle was freedom to the hills and vehicle to explore the back country around Grand Forks. I didn't have a driver's licence but that didn't stop me from going and exploring. I would go over dirt roads and paths and follow the side of a paved road to escape the possibility of being caught by police. Once away from town and paved roads I was free to ride unencumbered. Once I did caught by the police and got a stern talking to and had to push my bike back home. I put my black helmet on and jumped on my bike one afternoon. My left foot quickly kick started my motorcycle and it purred away. One down and four up were the gears that I maneuvered with the front of my right boot. My right hand quickly accelerated the throttle and I was off.

I drove down middle of the paved 17th street with not a care in the world. As I was passing the intersection of 17th street and 77th avenue I spotted two police cars at a house on the corner. The police men were standing outside by their cars and watched me drive by. I tried to nonchalantly nod to acknowledge them as I drove by, but realized my mistake. As I drove past them they noticed I had no licence plate on the rear of my cycle. One of the officers jumped in his car and the chase began. I quickly accelerated my bike in an attempt to outrun the police car. I raced up the hill at the end of 17th street and turned left on a dirt road just behind McCallum drive. The dirt road was full of pot holes and I remember turning around to see the police car and the officer bouncing up and down wildly as they were chasing me. I turned west on Coalshute road and raced to the intersection of Hardy Mountain and North Fork roads. I went straight through the intersection and flew up Hardy Mountain Road in an attempt to escape to the back roads of Hardy Mountain. The cop finally caught me half way to the top of the mountain. He was half amused but stern when he realized I was an underage adolescent. He gave me a stern talking to and mentioned fines and jail. He asked for my name and address and told me to push my bike home. And if he ever caught me again driving on the roads without a licence I would be in big trouble.

I didn't ride my bike for a while after that, but got restless as the forest and hills were beckoning to me. In grade 10 a new girl started to attend classes at Grand Forks Secondary School. Her name was Maggie and I heard she was from Vancouver. She had dirty blond shoulder length hair and bright emerald eyes. She lived at the Hardy Mountain School and looked as fresh as the mountain air that surrounded her. Rumour had it that she got into trouble in Vancouver and her parents decided to send to the Hardy Mountain School for remedial work. I thought she was pretty and we shared some classes together. I was a shy, nerdy kid who was a little socially awkward at this point of my life. I didn't really talk to her. I decided to take my bike and go explore around the vicinity of Hardy Mountain School and see if I could run into her there. I would spend countless hours exploring the back roads at the top of Hardy Mountain. I would go as far as Lost Lake way at the top of the mountain. I would go explore beyond the BC Hydro powerlines and far down the other side of the mountain to Highway 33 and cross over and go to Phoenix. Once I decided to stop in the school and visit. I got to have tea and tour there and met most of the people there. I befriended a younger guy named Mike. We shared some of the same interests of the outdoors and hung around together for a while. I never did see Maggie there and we never really connected. She was like some forbidden and exotic fruit that I was too scared to try. After high school I heard she moved back to Vancouver and became a nurse. We are friends on Facebook now.

Loresa, Tamara and Michelle from Hardy Mountain

In grade 12 I took a full complement of science courses including biology, chemistry and physics. I hung around the academic part of school and met a younger grade 11 student named Tanya. She had radiant skin, a cherubic face and a bouffant hairdo. And she was smart. Her dad was a teacher at the school, but that didn't stop me from asking her out.

The first car I ever owned as an AMC Gremlin. My dad decided that I should have a car. In grade 11, my dad bought it for me without my consultation. At first I was happy and excited to have my own vehicle. It was purple and had a big round glass window on the back of the car that looked like an upside down fish bowl. When I got the car I meticulously cleaned the car with the skill of a janitor. When my friend Anthony stopped by and saw what I was doing, he laughed and said that I was crazy. He said it was a Gremlin and it didn't matter. In a week it would be littered with fast food wrappers and pop bottles. In a way I guess he was right.

My first date was with Tanya and my Gremlin. I drove to her home by the Carson border in the country. My car was spotlessly cleaned and smelled of too much cheap aftershave. There was a long slightly slanting dirt road driveway to her house. I drove up and parked my car and went to knock on their front door. Her parents came out to greet me and then she followed. As we were doing introductions Tanya's mother pointed out that my car was slowly going backwards down the driveway. In my exuberance to be punctual and impress my date, I forget to put my car in park and put the emergency brake on. I quickly raced to recover my car and park it properly. No damage was done, other than to my ego. They invited me inside for juice and a snack.

It was a beautiful, warm summer's night. Commencing on our date, I drove to Christina Lake to go have dinner at the Time and Place Restaurant. After our meal I drove to Texas Point Park. I found a picnic bench overlooking the lake. I spread out checkered table cloth and brought out a bottle of wine and desert. We talked about school, life and our futures. After that we drove around and tried to find an outdoor party to go to. We had a good time that evening and I took her back home. On another date, I took Tanya to a movie at the Gem Theatre. We watched the show and we held hands. After the show finished we went back outside to find that somebody stuffed a garbage can in the front seat of my Gremlin. I was annoyed and mortified. I later discovered that my friends including Anthony, Ken and Warren were responsible for the devious act in an attempt to embarrass me when I was on a date.

I asked Tanya to be my date to the graduation ceremonies towards the end of my grade 12 year. She agreed and I was delighted. She wore a lovely peach coloured dress with frills and lace. She had her hair professionally styled. She looked beautiful. I wore a tight cream coloured suit and slacks with a freshly pressed light blue shirt and tie. We went together to the high school, but got separated during all the pomp and pageantry. Plenty of pictures were snapped and the whole evening was magical and fast. We slipped out of the uncomfortable attire and headed to the outdoor grad party at the motor cross tracks. There was a huge bonfire, some booze and a lot of raucous young adults. I stayed out the whole night and went home in the morning at sunrise. Tanya stayed at the party for a while and went home when her parents picked her up.

After I went to college and university I didn't see Tanya that much. Her family moved to Castlegar and she also went to a different university. She became a teacher, got married and had several children. I heard she became the vice-prinicipal and then principal of a large high school. We stayed friends.

After I went away to university in Vancouver and Seattle, I would return to Grand Forks in the summer to work and save money. One night after work I went out to socialize with a friend at the Yale Hotel Pub in downtown Grand Forks. There I met a beautiful, blond nurse who was a sister to one of my sister's friends. We hit it off, became friends and dated while I was still attending school. I later graduated from school, got married to Natalie, settled down in Kelowna, and had two children and a cat and a dog.

CHAPTER 11

Bill Barlee and Jolly Jack's Lost Gold Mine

I first learned about the legend of Jolly Jack's lost gold mine when I read the 1974 winter edition (Vol. 5 No. 1) of Canada West magazine. On pages 14 to 23 was an interesting article written by N.L. Barlee called Jolly Jack's Placer. I was intrigued to learn about a lost placer gold mine located somewhere between Rock Creek and Grand Forks. I was inspired to begin my quest to try find this hidden treasure.

John (Jack) Thornton was born June 11, 1824 in Durham County, England. In 1838, at the tender age of 14 years he left his home and decided to become a sailor. For 6 years he travelled across the Atlantic Ocean and explored the new world. He sailed to New York, Philadelphia, New Orleans and parts of the Caribbean. In 1844 he joined the United States Navy and was posted out of Boston. He sailed as far south as Chile in South America and made his way to California. In 1848 he heard about the California Gold Rush and sailed to San Francisco. In 1858, he heard about the Fraser River Gold Rush and he made his way north to Canada. In 1859, he went to Rock Creek. In 1860, he made his way south to the Columbia River near Marcus, Washington. He operated a successful placer gold operation there before returning to Canada. In Colville, he met and married Louise Polly Busch. For many years, they worked side by side on his claims. They had 13 children together, however 7 died and there remained 4 girls and 2 boys. They moved back to Canada and explored around Fort Steele, the Pend O'reille and Tulameen rivers.

Sometime in the 1880's, they set up their homestead on Boundary Creek between Greenwood and Midway. They built a cabin and later a house near where Norwegian Creek enters Boundary Creek. Jack prospected and mined in the summer and trapped in the winter. He would go with his old horse Rosie early in the morning and return later at night.

Sometimes he returned empty handed and other times he returned with some gold. It was during one of his trips that he returned with a baking powder can full of gold nuggets. He was wild with excitement and proclaimed to his wife that he finally struck it rich. Some of the gold nuggets were as large a walnut and close to an ounce in weight. The gold had a distinctive red or dark copper colour and was coarse and chunky. Many times he would leave in the early morning and return with a small sack of gold. He never would divulge the location of his find, not even to his wife. He was generally a talkative and gregarious person and earned the nickname Jolly Jack. He was also fond of whiskey and other spirits. He clammed up and remained tight-lipped to his friends and other patrons of saloons he frequented when asked about his gold mine. At the time it is believed that he pulled out about $60,000 from his secret mine. In today's currency, this would probably be worth well over a million dollars.

Jolly Jack Thornton continued to prospect well past 70 years of age before his failing health hampered him. With advanced age and poor health he moved to a home in Kamloops. His wife and his six children moved to Boundary Falls where she worked and the children attended school. John Thornton died on April 3, 1903 and he took the location of his gold mine with him to his grave. Over the years many other prospectors, amateur treasure hunters and history aficionados have tried and failed to find Jolly Jack's lost gold mine.

N.L. (Bill) Barlee was a clever raconteur and gifted story teller. He was also an avid historian, teacher, author, writer, publisher, museum curator, artifact collector, television host, politician and entrepreneur. He was passionate about the history of the old west and turn of the century historical sites, cities and mines throughout the Boundary country and beyond. He brought to life the old west and the colourful characters that inhabited it. He had a dynamic personality and charm, a sharp mind, wonderful sense of humour and a contagious laugh. He had an irrepressible passion and joy for life.

Neville Langrell (N.L.) Barlee was born on October 15, 1932 in Grand Forks, British Columbia during the great depression. His dad called him Bill. His family later moved to Rossland where he was raised. His grandfather operated a general store at Cascade City, a turn of the century CPR railway town located 6 kilometres south of Christina Lake at Cascade Falls on the Kettle River. Bill spent the bulk of his youth roaming around

Cascade City and other ghost towns and mining camps throughout the Boundary Country. He developed a keen interest in the local history that surrounded him. He visited towns like Gladstone, Niagara, Eholt, Phoenix, Greenwood, Deadwood, Anaconda, Rock Creek and Camp McKinney. From 1950 to 1970 he travelled around the Pacific Northwest and spent time in Alberta, British Columbia, Washington, Idaho and Montana. Bill then studied history at university and became a teacher. He taught high school in Penticton for 17 years. He taught History, Social Studies and Physical Education.

In 1969 he started Canada West Magazine. It was a magazine with a light tan cover, faded old west typewriter font type and black and white pictures. The early issues were 36 pages long. He did not want to compromise the integrity of the magazine and did not accept advertising. He did not accept subscriptions from the United States. He felt that many Americans were pillaging Canadian historical sites and he did not want to support this. The magazine had articles on ghost towns, general history, landmarks, gold creeks, authentic treasures and lost mines. It also had stories on flora and fauna, historical trails, Indian artifacts, campsites, bottle regions, famous characters, gemstones and a host of other related topics. He started with 7 paid subscribers and sold each magazine for 75 cents per copy. The magazine went on to have a circulation of 4000 copies per issue and have 1600 paid subscribers. He published the magazine quarterly for 6 or 7 years. In 1975 he sold the magazine to Garnet Basque. He bought it back in 1980 and published a few more issues. He then sold it back to Basque in 1985.

Bill Barlee also published at least 10 books. His first book was Similkameen: Pictograph Country in 1963. He self-published the book in the same large size as his magazine with a tan cover, faded print and black and white photographs. The book sold over 6000 copies. He wrote and published his second book, The Guide to Gold Panning in British Columbia. He then wrote and published the book Gold Creeks and Ghost Towns in 1973. He used to carry copies of his book along with him when he was travelling throughout the countryside. The book was very successful and he went on to sell over 100,000 copies. He later wrote several other books, including Historical Treasures and Lost Mines, The Prospectors and Collectors Guide, South Okanagan: Sagebrush Country, West Kootenay: Gold Town Country, Gold Creeks and Ghost Towns of Northeastern Washington and The Best Of Canada West.

Bill Barlee was a savvy politician. He was a member of the New Democrat Party and later the Liberal Party. He called himself an entrepreneur with a social conscience. He made two unsuccessful attempts to get elected into provincial politics before 1986. He then was elected as a member of the legislative assembly (MLA) of British Columbia in 1988 for the riding Boundary-Similkameen. He served until 1991 whereupon he was re-elected to the provincial legislature in 1991 for the riding Okanagan-Boundary and further served until 1996. From 1991 to 1993 he was appointed as Minister of Agriculture for the provincial government. He was later appointed as Minister of Tourism in 1993 and further served until 1996. As Minister of Agriculture he instituted the "Buy BC" slogan that encouraged British Columbians to buy agriculture that was locally produced from British Columbia farmers. The program was highly successful and the "Buy BC" slogan and logo is still used today. As Ministry of Tourism he championed the preservation of many British Columbia Historical sites. He was instrumental in helping the preservation of the old Kettle Valley railway. This railway corridor is used by tourists for biking and hiking as an important historical site in the Okanagan and Boundary Country. Bill made an unsuccessful attempt to get re-elected to the provincial government in 1996 losing the contest by a mere 27 votes to the liberal candidate. He then made an unsuccessful attempt to run in federal politics under the liberal party in 2000. Afterwards, he retired from active politics.

In 1986, Bill became co-host of the widely successful CHBC Television show Gold Trails and Ghost Towns with Okanagan weatherman Mike Roberts. The modestly produced series showed Bill dressed in jeans and a jean jacket sitting discussing the history of a ghost town, lost gold mine or some other turn of the century historical interest. Mike would ask him question or show him an artifact and Bill would then go eloquently and passionately on to explain the topic in great detail. He would recall times, dates and faces with uncanny precision and clarity. He was a master story teller and he explained his stories in ways that were appealing and intriguing for the audience. He told interesting stories and often intertwined humour and historical facts. The show would display many old black and white photographs of old cities, buildings, mines and colourful characters. The show ran for 10 years until 1996. About 13 episodes were produced per year. The show was picked up by 5 different networks across Canada and had up to 200,000 viewers per episode.

Bill was also an entrepreneur and prospector. He owned several claims including placer gold and platinum mines. He was an expert gold panner and he won several gold panning contests. Some of his ventures were successful while others were not. He was passionate about preserving areas and objects of historical interest. It was is said that he amassed a collection of over 15,000 artifacts of the old west throughout the years. Many of his collections were on display at museums including the British Columbia Provincial Museum in Victoria and the Museum of Civilization in Ottawa, Ontario. He was also a museum curator. He owned and operated Bill Barlee's Museum of the Old West in Penticton and Summerland. He tried to preserve an old ghost town called Sandon near Nakusp. In the 1970's, he invested considerable time and money in trying to convert Sandon into the next preserved ghost town, like Barkerville. He purchased an entire block of the old Sandon city in the hopes of preserving the old buildings. But lack of investors and heavy snowfall contributed to the demise of the project and collapse of many of the old buildings.

Bill was also very competitive and was an accomplished athlete. He played hockey, lacrosse and tennis. He was fast and wiry. When he was a young man he ran the mile in a time that set the record in the Okanagan Valley which lasted for 20 years. He also won singles and double titles in tennis throughout the Okanagan. He enjoyed beating competitors in tennis who were 20 to 30 years his junior. N.L. (Bill) Barlee passed away June 14, 2012 in Victoria, British Columbia.

In my earlier years, I met Bill Barlee two times. I would go the Mir Bookstore on Market Street in Grand Forks when I was a teenager. I picked up copies of Canada West Magazine. I was intrigued by his explanation about old ghost towns, mines and lost treasures around the Boundary Country. I purchased his books Gold Creeks and Ghost Towns and the Guide to Gold Panning in British Columbia. I studied them and read them several times. I purchased steel gold pans from the White Elephant Store in Spokane, Washington. I set about exploring old ghost towns and gold creeks around Grand Forks. Images and visions of lost treasure, gold coins and lost mines swirled around in my head.

When I was a teenager, I met Bill Barlee the first time. Somehow I phoned him and we met him at an old historical house in downtown

Uncle Mickey the Barber

Grand Forks. I presumed the house was his or in his family. It was on 3rd or 4th street just off 75th Avenue behind the Overwaitea grocery store. He was a tall, slim man wearing jeans, a plaid shirt and jean jacket. He had a slightly receding hairline and wore large Dark glasses. We had a cup of tea. He talked fast and was very knowledgeable and informative. He knew a lot about the local history. I was spellbound listening to his captivating stories. I sat there in awe. I asked him some questions and he seemed to have all the answers. I asked him about the location of Jolly Jack's lost placer gold mine. He wouldn't say for sure, but he thought it was on Skeff Creek, a tributary of July Creek. After our short, cordial visit, I thanked him and said good bye.

The second time I met Mr. Barlee was a about year later. I was still searching for Jolly Jack's lost placer mine. I had spent time exploring the areas west of Highway 33 on the way to Greenwood just past Spencer's Hill. I would drive along the old gravel roads that traversed Gibbs Creek, May Creek and July Creek. I would try my hand at gold panning and set up a small, wooden sluice box. On one occasion a friend and I took my dad's old pickup and drove up to Skeff Creek. We drove a short distance off the highway and stumbled upon a derelict mining operation with no one around. There were a couple of big holes and large piles of dirt around the creek that turbulently cascaded down the side of the hill. There was a small bull dozer, a large metallic sluice box and an abandoned trailer. We started exploring the site and eagerly wondered if we had found Jolly Jack's lost placer mine. Then all of a sudden we heard the noise of a vehicle approaching. Out of a big truck jumped a man that looked like Grizzly Adams. He was a big, burly man with suspenders and a thick red flannel shirt. He had a full beard and long wavy white hair. He asked us what we were doing there and he was suspicious of us. We heard another vehicle approaching. It was a small, dark Toyota truck. The door opened and out jumped Bill Barlee. He recognized me and helped defuse the situation with Grizzly Adams. Bill said that he was just passing through and decided to stop at Skeff Creek. He said that we were probably close to the location where Jolly Jack Thornton was believed to have his placer gold mine. The gold extracted from this location shared the same colour and physical characteristics as that of Jolly Jack's gold. He explained that Grizzly Adams owned the claim and operation here and we should be careful about exploring around this location. We had a short visit with Bill and Grizzly Adams, then quickly made our retreat.

When I was a teenager growing up in Grand Forks, Bill Barlee and his books greatly influenced and inspired me. I learned a lot about the local history of Grand Forks and the Boundary Country. I explored gold creeks and ghost towns, I searched for treasures and lost mines and I imagined how life was in the old west at the turn of the century. I am thankful I was able to meet Mr. Barlee and read his books. To this day, I am still not really quite sure if I did stumble across Jolly Jack Thornton's lost gold mine or not.

CHAPTER 12

GFSS and Other Social Deviations

Grand Forks Secondary School or GFSS was a collection of large grey buildings on Central Avenue in the middle of Grand Forks. No building was taller than two stories. There was a main entrance in the middle that leads to the central office. There were a whole bunch of classrooms on the left side that housed the academic department. There was a library in the middle that faces the outside opposite the office. There was a 500 seat auditorium on the right side for drama classes and also doubled as a community gathering centre. The gymnasium is on the right side in the back of the building behind the auditorium. Behind the main building were the shop classes including drafting, mechanics, metalwork and woodworking. Behind the shop building was a grassy field for physical education classes. It was where I went to high school for five years from grades 8 to 12. Like the cliché from the Charles Dickens novel a Tale of Two Cities, "It was the best of times and it was the worst of times."

At first it was difficult navigating through new shorter classes with different teachers, meeting new people and adjusting to new expectations. Unlike elementary school you didn't stay in the same class and have the same teacher all day. You moved around. With the bell you shuffled to new classes at different parts of the school with different teachers. These new teachers had higher expectations for you. Unlike elementary school you were encouraged to study and do some homework. You were expected to work a little harder. Courses would build upon each other. One course would lead to another. In the upper grades after grade 10, you could choose own courses. You were encouraged to make a decision as to your future vocation after high school. You were on the pathway to your future.

In high school you had a little more pressure to fit in and figure out who you were. There was expectations to do well academically and succeed in things that interested and challenged you. In high school you were encouraged to address parts of your expanding life that you struggled with, didn't make sense or needed an adjustment. There was peer pressure to experiment with drugs and alcohol which were both freely available. There was peer pressure to engage with the opposite sex. If you had a problem you were encouraged to talk to your peers and teachers. High school was a time of rapid change and growth. You were encouraged to embrace the growth. My time at high school was a fun time of growth, learning and adventure.

In grade 8, going to high school seemed like a daunting experience at first. It seemed overwhelming and uncomfortable. At first it was difficult navigating through new shorter classes with different teachers, meeting new people and adjusting to new expectations. You moved around. With the bell you shuffled to new classes at different parts of the school with different teachers. You took basic classes like English, Math, Science and Social Studies. I generally liked school, tried hard and did well at all my classes. I don't remember much about grade 8, except for trying to stay out of the way of the older, bigger kids. My favorite class that year was the English class taught by Mr. McRae.

I hung out with a group of friends who shared the same age, common interests and goals as I. You just seemed to naturally gravitate to some people and form a bond. There were different cliques and groups in high school. There were the cool guys, the jocks, the nerds and the losers. The girls were even more vicious in their social inclinations and hung around in their tightly formed groups. I hung out with a group of friends including Tony, Darrell, Jeff, Kevin, Landon, Marcus, Nelson and Walter. There were others who came and went, but we formed a close social nucleus. We hung out together in the hallways and talked about school, life and girls, before, after and between classes. We sat near each other in classes and shared secret handshakes, personalized nuances and idiosyncratic quirks. We phoned each other and socialized together when we weren't in classes. We were a posse of unrequited teen energy and angst. Looking back I think we were the group of average guys. We were average cool, average jocks and smart, but not too smart.

Tony had the nickname Toes. I am really not sure why we called them that. He was pretty fast with his fingers and was nimble on his toes. His dad worked as a drywaller and Tony inherited and learned his dad's work ethic. He was fast, strong and worked hard. I remember putting up drywall on a ceiling with him. It was hard to keep up with him. We played together in the 3 on 3 basketball tournament in high school. I missed an easy shot at the end and we lost the game.

Darrell was the oldest son of my favorite hockey coach. We played hockey together and he had a nice place at Christina Lake. He was a transplant from Vancouver who wanted to be a mechanic like his dad. He was tall and slim, had a good sense of humour and the girls seemed to like him.

Jeff was my friend who lived across from grandmother's house in west Grand Forks. When I was young I used to play with him and his older brother Ian. He was good at most sports and pretty smart too. His mother was a teacher and his dad lived in Vancouver. We used to hang out in his basement watching sports like football and hockey. It was a good, safe place to chill and sit around on his couch. I blew up a chemistry set in the foyer of his house once. I stuck a cork on a flask of some liquid that I then put on a Bunsen burner. I seemed to forget that liquids expand and create gas when heated. I left the concoction on the burner and then went to do something else. The whole thing exploded and left distinctive green blotches all over their ceiling tiles. His mom came home and scolded me, but she seemed to be unrealistically relaxed about the affair.

Kevin was one of my best friends. He played hockey and was pretty good, but he lacked some size. He was very competitive at all sports and just about everything else. He liked to win and didn't like to lose. His older cousin Brian was a great hockey player with whom we played on with the Grand Forks Border Bruins. In high school Kevin had a high pitched squeaky voice. Most of the members of your group would make fun of him about this once in a while. Kevin used to have a maroon coloured little Datsun truck. I remember we used to drive around in circles up and down Central Avenue many times on Friday and Saturday nights looking for girls and a party to go to.

Landon was Jeff's cousin. He was quiet, reserved and thoughtful. He wasn't quite as loud and outlandish as some of the other guys in our group. He really respected his dad who was the manager of one of the mills in Grand Forks. His family used to own a cabin on Christina Lake by Texas Point. In summertime I would occasionally go there and hang out. It was beautiful on the lake and we went swimming, tubing and waterskiing. Sometimes we used to go hiking up McRae Creek in the mountains behind their cabin. There was an area down a steep embankment on the creek called the Potholes. It was a slab of pure granite carved out by the creek. The fast cascading water would swirl around the granite potholes like a whirlpool. You could lower yourself down into the creek and sit in these whirlpools. It was cool and refreshing.

Marcus was a friend who lived in Ruckle Addition. His father died when he was young and he was raised along with his sisters by his single mother. He was pretty smart and had a good sense of humour. We used to go swimming at his sister's Elaine's place and have parties there. We went to Selkirk College together after we graduated from high school. We lived together in some apartments called the Chicken Coop in Robson. I played a joke on him once there that he didn't seem to like. When he was at his classes I put his bed on the roof of our place. I thought it was really funny. He was pissed off and wasn't amused.

Nelson became the prime minister of our high school. We played hockey together for many years. His family owned and operated a jewelry and gift store in downtown Grand Forks. They lived in a neat place up the North Fork dump side. Nelson liked fast cars and loud rock music. I remember I first heard Jim Croce's Time in a Bottle at his place. Nelson once had this old car called a Ford Anglia. Nelson, Jeff, Marcus and I took a trip in his Anglia to a Barter fair that was occurring at July Creek Ranch in the woods just outside Grand Forks. We drove together in this small car and I remember it barely made it up Spencer's Hill. When we got there it was like no country fair I had ever seen before. There were beatniks, hippies and dropouts. The air was full of the aroma of cannabis and incense. Women with braided hair danced in scantily clad clothes to the beat of 1960's music. Long haired men with unshaven beards walked around shirtless, in overalls or even wearing animal skins. We stayed there for a while then made a hasty retreat back to reality.

Nick had the nickname Hutch. I think he earned that named because he looked like one of the characters in the show Starsky and Hutch. He was quiet and had a good sense of humour. The girls seemed to like him and he always seemed to have a pretty girlfriend.

Uncle Mickey the Barber

Walter was a pretty smart guy who was good at electronics. He was fun, active and liked to do things. He used to have a sauna at his house. He used to invite some friends over and we would play pool and have a hot sweat in his sauna. He could be a little meddlesome at times. I remember once sleeping at home on Friday night when I heard a loud rapping on my window. It was Walter and it was 2 o'clock in the morning. Apparently he drove his Toyota Celica car off the road at the intersection of Donaldson Drive and North Fork Road. It had snowed and granted it was slippery, but he wanted me to tow him out with my dad's truck. I obliged and went there to help him till the police showed up.

We were a rag tag group of friends who were looking for fun and excitement. We used to go out together to shows at the Gem theatre together. We sat around booths of restaurants like Sheila's and Big T wasting time, chatting about nonsense and eating French fries. We talked about girls, school and more about girls. We went to many parties together, some indoor parties at somebody's house and some outdoor parties with big bonfires and loud music. We helped each other out most of the time with our unwritten bond and code of conduct. Most of the time we got along, but sometimes we would disagree and fight. Through thick and thin we were a pretty close group of high school friends.

Grade 9 was a continuation of the previous grade. I was feeling adjusted and little more comfortable with high school life. I liked school, was doing well in my classes and seemed to fit in easier. You continued with basic classes like English, Math, Science and Social Studies. The teachers were generally good and conscientious. The worst thing about grade 9 was when my mom permed my straight hair. She thought it was a good idea and would make me look cute. I had curls after the treatment that lasted three months. All my friends in the group teased me endlessly.

Grade 10 was a continuation of the previous grade except for one thing. You could get your driver's license when you turned 16 years old. It was an important rite of passage in you teenage years. It marked the time when you were almost an adult. You were given the privilege and responsibility to drive on the roads of the province with unbridled enthusiasm and cautious vigilance. GFSS had a big parking lot full of hot cars. The automobile you drove was a status symbol that reflected your personality. There were cool muscle cars like Chevrolet Camaros, Dodge Chargers, Ford Mustangs and Pontiac Trans AM. They had big engines, sounded powerful and were often painted in bright attractive colours. My dad bought me a purple AMC Gremlin. It was a compact car that looked up upside down fish bowl. It competed with the Ford Pinto and Chevrolet Vega as the worst car available for teenagers. It was partially responsible for my ruined social life. I called my purple AMC Gremlin the Anti-Christ. It reflected by disdain and relationship with this vehicle and its mechanical reliability. However, I was appreciative it did get me from point A to point B and back again.

In grade 11 I decided I wanted to pursue academic courses in preparation of attending college and university in the future. I took a full course load with Biology, Chemistry, English, Math and Physics. I started wearing glasses at this time and I walked around with a whole bunch of big textbooks under my arm. I spent most of my time in the science area of the school and saw a little less of my regular friends. I loved learning about the sciences and soaked up the material with eager abandon. My Physics teacher was Mr. G. He lived in Belgium during World War II and still couldn't get over his memories of the war. He wore big glasses, was stern and had a quirky sense of humour. Mr. C. was my Chemistry teacher who lived on a hobby farm near Christina Lake. He had was always pleasant and smiling and reminded me of a friendly puppy. Mr. S. was my biology teacher. Some of the students nicknamed him Screwy. He meant well and told a lot of stories about his life. I can remember one story he told us when he was a young child. He lost his mittens in a school field in the middle of wintertime. His mean father made him go outside in the cold, snowy weather and not come back till he found them. Mr. M. was my math teacher who talked like a computer. I remember one saying he said almost every class, "make sure your brain is in gear, before mouth is motion." I took some elective shop courses to help balance the academic sciences. I especially liked woodwork and electricity. Mr. P. was my teacher for both courses. He used to call me Lobes for short. I built a canoe, a desk and a waterbed in woodwork class. I remember one time I was late getting back from lunch for his class and I had to get a late slip in the office. I just made up a stupid excuse that my mom's vacuum cleaner was blocking the door and I had to wait for her to finish. He thought that was hilarious and would remind me years later of that creative, lame excuse.

Sometimes I would hang out with some of the older kids that I seemed to get along with. Steve was a grade older than me and we had a

95

lot in common. We both liked the outdoors, biking and played hockey. He was very strong and agile. We went hiking together on some arduous and strenuous adventures. We would bike around the North Fork loop. He had powerful legs and was often ahead of me. When I worked for the Grand Forks Art Gallery, I cleverly organized a fundraising trip whereby I would go on bike trip to raise money for a wheel chair ramp.

I decided to bike from Jasper, Alberta to Grand Forks and asked Steve to come with me. My brother dropped us off in Jasper and we camped out and started cycling home the next day. Steve bicycled like he was in the Tour de France and I followed behind him. My sprocket broke on a steep hill near the Columbia Ice Fields. I thumbed a ride to Banff to get a new bike and caught up with Steve a short time later. We had a wonderful time cycling together through the Rocky Mountains and back to Grand Forks. We had some other epic journeys together including climbing Mount Adams in southern Washington State. I also hung around with Jamie. He was a year older. His older brother was friends with my older brother. Jamie's mother, who was a teacher, passed away when Jamie was young. He lived with his dad near the hospital. They had a pool in their back yard and they had some fun parties there. Jamie was pretty smart and athletic. We used to go together as a team in the Lions Club Raft Race for a few years. We also went to Selkirk College and the University of British Columbia at the same time.

In grade 12 I continued to take academic courses including Biology, Chemistry, English, Math and Physics in preparation of college and university. I still enjoyed school, but was happy it was finishing and I could move on. At this time I was on the student council with Nelson, Marlene and Sandy. I was host of the annual end of year Awards Banquet in the auditorium with all the students in our school. I was also busy applying for scholarships and different schools to go to. The excitement of graduation came and went quickly. I woke up one morning a little older. I was finished high school, made it through GFSS unscathed and enjoyed the whole process.

CHAPTER 13

Fred W. and Mr. H.

I have had many teachers throughout my education experience. Some have been good, a few poor and most of the rest have been mediocre. I have been through 12 years of elementary and high school. I have been through 8 years of college and university. I have a Bachelor of Science degree in Biology and Chemistry from the University of British Columbia in Vancouver. I have a Doctorate in Naturopathic Medicine from Bastyr College of Natural Health Sciences in Seattle, Washington. I have taken numerous post-graduate courses and seminars. I have seen a lot of teachers.

I had this one poor teacher for my third year Genetics course at the University of British Columbia. It was a large class of over 300 students held in a large slanting auditorium. He was a tall, slim man who wore large glasses and had blonde wavy hair and a bald spot at the top of his head. He spoke from the podium as I sat above with the others in the rafters. He spoke in a long, boring monotone voice occasionally looking up from the overhead projector. I just couldn't understand what he was saying. It didn't make sense. I knew Genetics would be a hard course, but I just couldn't connect the dots. The light in my head was not turning on. I couldn't understand the principles of what he was saying. I asked other students sitting to the right and left of me if they understood what the professor was taking about. They were as confused as me and said "no." I asked other students in the hallway after class if they understood what he was saying. Almost all of them said "no, I don't understand." I decided to make an appointment to see the professor himself and asked explain to me what he was talking about. I said to him 'I don't understand what you are saying in class." He said that makes two of us, "I don't understand what I am saying half the time either." He continued, "You see I am a researcher and I am only teaching this course to get grants to continue my research and I don't even really know what I am talking about." I thought dumbfounded, "Well doesn't that just about explains everything" and thanked him and left.

What makes a great teacher? Every one of us remembers that one special teacher in elementary, middle or high school. That teacher made a strong impact on our education and lasting impact our lives. We remember him or her twenty or even thirty years later. They inspired and motivated you to learn. They helped you believe in yourself and develop your self-confidence. They had life experience and shared their findings with you. They have made mistakes and allowed you to make mistakes too. They inspired and engaged you to do your best. They brought out passion and work ethic in you. They had high expectations for you and helped you dream big. For you, that one special teacher made learning fun and rewarding.

Teaching is a complicated art. It requires a combination of knowledge of subject matter with passion for learning and teaching. It utilizes an understanding of curriculum with good, effective communication. It needs strong support while building trusting, caring relationships. It requires organization, classroom management and moderate discipline. It stimulates an eagerness to learn, engages students in critical thinking and shows different points of view. It displays a willingness to reflect and a change when necessary. Teaching requires a passion for life and learning and a love of people and students.

Fred W. as my math teacher in high school at GFSS or Grand Forks Secondary School. I had him for several classes and enjoyed my time with him. Math was a pure science with only one right answer. The beauty is the simplicity of the outcome. You are either right or wrong. There are no shades of grey in math. Of course you would have to exercise your brain to figure out the right answer. There are different parts of math including algebra, geometry, probability and statistics to name a few. I liked all different parts of math and I had a great teacher to help me along the way.

Fred W. was a big, rotund man who sweat on his forehead when he walked upstairs to his second floor math class. He rode a motorcycle to school and looked a little disheveled and offsetting with his shirt sticking out of the back of his baggy pants. He talked in a methodical and analytical slightly higher pitched voice. He wore black glasses and had

Fred W. and Mr. H.

dark wavy hair. He liked to bring his coffee cup with him from the staff room at the start of class. I also seen him smoking. He coached both the girls and boys basketball teams in high school. I don't think he was much of athlete and he wasn't in the greatest physical shape. Players liked him and listened to him. He explained things very well, laid out his demands and expectations clearly and was good at motivation. He had good success coaching because he was a good teacher.

In math class he spoke clearly and explained things with resounding clarity. He made good use of the blackboard. He would draw out and explain the lesson we were on. He would outline the steps required to solve the problem. He would only use the necessary and relevant facts. He would eliminate jargon and inapplicable blather. He would then explain what was expected of us and what assignment was due. He was practical and pragmatic. He would allow us to work in class. He was firm and stern yet somewhat accommodating. If somebody was wasting time or talking when not allowed, he would let them know. I saw him throw the chalk he was writing with at the wall only once when he was pissed off at somebody for not listening. His tests were fair and honest.

Looking back, there was nothing obviously special or unique about Fred, except that he had a good way of explaining things. He had a teaching style that resonated with me. His classroom was plain and simple. His desk was ordinary and uncluttered. He explained things clearly. He laid out his demands and expectations. He let his students do their work independently. He would walk around the classroom and help you if you asked him. He didn't belittle or put anybody down. He treated with respect and courtesy. He didn't reward his students with stupid drivel. He didn't gloss over and sugar coat things. I remember his favorite saying that I often heard, but didn't grasp the full meaning of. He said, "You know kids, it's not easy out there." Only later in life did I understand the meaning of his sage advice.

Mr. H. was another exceptional teacher that I crossed paths with. Mr. H was my daughter's grade 5 teacher at Kelowna Christian School. He was a slim, average height middle aged man with a bald spot on top of his head. He played guitar and sang in a church group on Sundays. He was nice, easy going and didn't yell in the classroom. And best of all, he gave candy in school to his students.

Mr. H. always had fun games and contests in the classroom. This made learning fun. To help his students learn Social Studies he invented a game called Social Jeopardy. This game was like the television show, Jeopardy, except all the questions were about what we were learning in Social Studies. The winner got a jar full of one hundred gummy worms. One time his class was allowed to have a water gun fight outside on a hot day in June. He brought the water guns and he even allowed his students to spray him with water. Another day he had a contest to see who were the best behaved and hardest working students. He would buy the winners a Blizzard ice cream treat from Dairy Queen. My daughter Sarah was one of them.

Mr. H. would have exciting activities in the classroom. This would get his students attention. Sometimes he would let them watch videos in class and eat popcorn. Other times he would play his guitar and get them to sing songs in the classroom. Another time he gave them real money from the African country of Zambia. He went to this poor country on a mission trip the summer before. He talked about his trip there. Once they made tie dyed t-shirts to learn about art and science. Another time he brought a video camera to class. They made movies in class like Nerd Idol and Darth Vador.

They had many fun class parties. This made his students work towards a goal. Mr. H. gave his class party points for good behavior. He would take away party points for bad behavior. When the class had 100 party points, they were allowed to have a party in class. Once they had a pizza party. He bought the pizza. Then they had a pajama party and dressed in pajamas at school for the whole day. Another time they had an ice cream party. He bought the ice cream. Another time they had a camping party. They set up small tents in the classroom, got in the tents and did school work there.

Mr. H. gave interesting tests in class. One time he gave his students a pop quiz. It had ten questions all about soda pop. Another time he warned his students that they were going to have the dreaded two hour multiple choices CAT test or the standardized Canadian Achievement Test. When it came time for the test, he gave them a test all about their knowledge about cats.

My daughter Sarah had some slight difficulties at school. She struggled with some of her academic classes like mathematics. Even from grade one she was identified out as a student who needed some extra help. Most of the time, she persevered and worked hard to get by. Other times she was frustrated and exasperated. Most teachers were helpful, understanding and sympathetic. Some teachers were rude, unapologetic and uninterested. There were special tests to assess her learning and comprehension. There were extra meetings to discuss her progress and growth. They were education strategies to help her learn better and quicker. There were adapted programs, modified goals and outcomes and individualized education plans. They were after class sessions and extra time to do work at home. Some strategies were helpful while others were not. Part of the time they undermined her confidence and hindered her progress. Even though she struggled, she was always inspired by a special teacher she once had in her grade five elementary school. He brought out the best in Sarah. He treated her nice and inspired her. He was always encouraging and accommodating. He made learning for her fun and interesting. She always tried her best and was excited about going to school. She will always remember him and we are forever thankful for him.

The quality of education a student receives is directly proportional to the quality of the teacher. Fred W. and Mr. H. were two examples of high quality teachers who exemplified what it was to be a great teacher. The inspired and motivated, encouraged and developed. Of course, they were also good at teaching. There were other teachers I have encountered who were also great teachers who made a lasting impact on my life. There was Mr. G. my physics teacher, Mr. C. my chemistry teacher and Mr. P. my woodwork teacher. They made a lasting, positive impression on my life. They were my best teachers ever.

CHAPTER 14

The Gazette, the Highways and the Forestry

Ever since I was 12 years old I worked at odd jobs in Grand Forks. My parents encouraged to get a job, work hard and make a little bit of money. It sounded like good advice, I had the time and I wanted to buy some things like candy, hockey sticks and shoes. Like most people I wasn't born with a silver spoon in mouth. I came from a regular working middle class family. My dad had a good job and he worked at the Department of Highways. He was shop foreman at the Grand Forks operation. My mom stayed home, cooked and cleaned and ran the house. She made sure our clothes were clean and we had food to eat. She also did yard work, sewed and grew a garden. Working was an indelible part of our life. We were allowed to have fun and a waste time, but we were also expected to work and be productive.

When I was 12 years old I get my first job delivering the Vancouver Province newspaper in the west end of Grand Forks. I used to deliver the newspaper early in the morning or the late afternoon. The job got boring in a hurry and I only did this for about 6 months. I got another job weeding onions in Hoffman's fields on Carson Road one summer. I would bike to the country with my lunch and water in the early morning and work a full day. We would work all day in the blazing sun. It was hot, dry and dirty work. There were about 20 other people working in the field at the same time. Sometimes we would talk to each other times not. Sometimes we would horse around and throw dirt bombs at each other. The supervisor was a short German guy named Herb with a thick accent. If we got caught fooling around we would reprimanded or even fired. He inspected our rows that we were weeding and see if we did a good job. The fields were big and he would have to drive around to the other end or another field. When he was gone everyone let up, took a break and lied down between the rows or just plain horsed around. We would have

The Gazette, the Highways and the Forestry

someone spot for Herb because sometimes he would stand up on the box of his truck peering with binoculars to see if we were still at work. Another job I got was mowing lawns and doing yard work for old people around the city. I would go to different places and clean the yard, weed the flower beds and remove grass and other refuse. It was a better job than delivering newspapers and weeding onions.

When I was fifteen years old I got a job working at the local newspaper called the Grand Forks Gazette. The office was located in an old brick building in the centre of town. I did odd jobs there including cleaning and janitorial work, collating and folding advertising flyers and helping upstairs with the print and layout of the newspaper. There was a huge old printing press in a room on the main floor that smelled pungent with the aroma of black ink. The old press used to lug away on printing flyers and other jobs for customers in a steady, predictable rhythm. The pressman was a nice old guy who did this for over forty years. The building had an old dusty and musty basement where the newspapers were folded and collated with flyers. I would use an old piece of broomstick handle to fold the papers to prevent my hands from getting covered in ink.

Stanley Orris was the publisher of the Gazette newspaper. He was an old, bespectacled bald curmudgeon with big glasses who used to like to smoke cigars. I got to know him quite well and he invited me over to his old stately heritage house by Perley School. He had a separate addition to his house that was for all the books he collected. He was supposed to have the largest, private library in Canada. He had a lot of books and he shared my passion for reading. He wrote his weekly column for the newspaper with his large old typewriter. I remember hearing the repetitive clack clack of the individual letters hitting the paper as he typed away. He encouraged me to write. I tried writing a sports column in the newspaper of activities in our high school. I also tried writing some short stories for a local historical publication. I even published a small historical and lifestyle magazine called the Kettle River Miner. I dropped some of the magazines off at stores throughout Grand Forks. I sold copies of the magazine for 25 cents back then. I even had one full time paid subscriber. Looking back now I realize that most of the stuff I produced was crap. It was wordy, flowery and confusing. I overused metaphors and misused similes. I was always trying to write like somebody else. I was even guilty of borderline plagiarism with some of the work I produced back then. I worked for about 2 years at the Gazette.

Uncle Mickey the Barber

When I was 17 years old he my dad got me a job working on a survey crew in the summer time. My dad was the shop foreman at the Department of Highways in Grand Forks. The survey crew was located at the main office of Central Avenue in Grand Forks across from the Overwaitea grocery store. The head surveyor was a short guy named Jack who talked with country drawl. He had dark hair, was really interested in local history and had a flatulence problem. He made his own home made beer and drank it after work and on hot days on the weekend. We would drive around to gravel pits around the Boundary Country and measure volumes. I was the rodman and I basically held a ten foot ruler and hiked up and down the sides gravel pit to take shots. Jack had a system of volume measurements that was perfected to an art. I would not more than three of four measurements per slice at the base, top and any unusual crest on the hill. It was quick and accurate. We had a lot of time to explore old historical sites around the Boundary Country. We also measured the topography and slopes of roads and curves around the road. I would pound colourful stakes in the ground with neon flagging and write important numbers on the side of the wood. Jack knew what he was doing and he adroitly measured what needed to measure with quick and rapid skill.

We had an old draftsman named Mike that sometimes came in the field with us. He was hard of hearing and got some things really mixed up. One time in between Rock Creek and Osooyos we were surveying the beautiful and grassy landscape south of Camp Mckinney. A stunning and friendly black lab would greet us each day. We didn't know his name and just called him Blackie. Mike couldn't hear clearly and got the name twisted around. He called the dog Blankey. Why would they call the dog Blankey he wondered? We would ask him about the dog and had an ongoing joke about this for several weeks afterward.

When Jack was in the office doing paperwork and drawings, I would join my cousin Rob on the survey crew. He was a junior surveyor below Jim in rank and seniority. He was also the union representative and seemed to know all the rules and regulations pertaining to working for the BC Government Employees Union. He stuck to the rules. For instance, he knew that for every two hours of employed work you were entitled to a 10 minute break. We would drive for two hours to the west end of the Boundary Country in Christian Valley in big old orange and white crew cab. He checked his watch and would pull over to the side of the road for a break and short snooze at precisely 2 hours. Needless to say I quickly learned how a cushy, union job worked. I would also doze off during many warm afternoons in the passenger seat of the vehicle when we were driving back from a worksite somewhere out in the field.

When I was 19 years old I got a job on the Initial Attack crew of the Ministry of Forests in Grand Forks. I was basically a firefighter for forest fires in the summer months. It was one of the best jobs a kid for wish for. We got specialized training in fire behavior and suppression. We got to use specialized equipment and operate big trucks with pumps and hoses. We wore special red or yellow fire retardant suites. We each had walkie-talkies and big, cumbersome portable phones. And the best part of all is that we got to fly in helicopters all around the Boundary Country. Our helicopter was a Bell Jet Ranger 206.

We were stationed next to the airport in Grand Forks so we could have quick access to the helicopter in case we had to go to a fire. They had a pilot who was on contract and who hung around the airport and his hotel room nearby. We had specialized training to enter and exit the helicopter safely. We would kneel together at a location where the pilot could visibly see us. The helicopter would nose in first before it would land and we would be on one of the sides of the aircraft closest to the front. The same was true for exiting the machine. In remote locations sometimes the helicopter couldn't land. The pilot would find a clear rocky outcrop and hover 3 to 6 feet off the ground. We would carefully undo our seat belts and climb to the edge of the craft. We would open the door and carefully step on the skids or side rails going backwards down on the inside of the rail and propel ourselves to the ground. We would then proceed to the front of the aircraft, kneel down and wait for rest of the passengers to exit. It was the duty of the pilot to maintain his stable and correct position while we were exiting. Once everybody was out our group leader would then give the thumbs up sign to the pilot and he would fly away.

I would almost feel like Tom Cruise in the movie Top Gun, except I wasn't actually flying the aircraft. In the helicopter we wore helmets with specialized headsets so we could communicate back and forth with each other. The helicopter had the distinctive colours of red, white and blue. The craft had six seats in three rows of two. Many times we would take the rear doors off the helicopter. We would be flying at 6,000 feet with the doors open and the pilot would bank and make a turn. We would be looking at an angle straight towards the ground below. There was

105

nothing separating you but some air and the seatbelt that held you in. It was exhilarating to be a part of the Initial Attack group and fly around the country.

At the base there were two initial attack groups of three individuals. Sometimes we all worked together but we were a distinct and separate entity who worked independently. In my group was our leader Jason, Warren and myself. Both Jason and Warren were older, but we got along well. Jason worked hard, played the guitar and seemed a little moody at times. Warren was a semi-retired professional ski instructor who lived in a cabin on Christina Lake. He liked to have fun and sold expensive sunglasses to me and my friends when we visited him at the lake. Cory was the leader of the other group. He was also a skier who was a little uptight, but would laugh occasionally when he dropped his guard. A lot of times we would compete with the other group to see who was faster or better at doing something. It kept us sharp and on our toes.

If there were no fires happening in our region, we would go out to do different odd jobs in the field. We would load up our crummy crew cab truck and leave the base in the morning. We kept close radio contact with the office in case something changed and we were needed to return to the base as soon as possible. We would drive out to some location in the forest and do some task or job that needed to be done. We did a lot of road brushing and clearing. Old seldom used forestry roads would become quickly overgrown by shrubs and trees and covered with rocks and other debris. We would high powered wiper snippers and use chainsaws to clear the way. We practiced falling dead trees that were consumed by decay or previous fire. We cleaned forestry campsites and parks. We would mark and flag trees that needed to be thinned and removed. We practiced using our pumps in creeks and ponds in the outback. I really enjoyed being outside in the forests and natural beauty around us.

We got to see many beautiful and refreshing sites throughout the Boundary Country. We used to go to Jewel Lake, Xenia Lake, Burrell Creek, Texas Creek and other attractive and alluring areas. One of my favorite places to go was the Bluejoint Lookout located over 60 kilometres up the North Forks in the Granby watershed and mountain range. There was an old forestry lookout and radio tower located at the top of Bluejoint Mountain. It was at an elevation slightly over 2000 metres or 6000 feet. Sometimes the helicopter would drop of us at the top of the mountain near the lookout. Other times we drove our crummy up the North Fork, park at the end of the access road halfway up the mountain and hike in the rest of the way. Our job was usually to cleanup, fix and repair the lookout. We did a little bit of carpentry work and painting. We were in the high alpine country and the chipmunks, pine siskins and stellar jays kept us company. Of course there were mosquitoes there. We would have the most sublime and expansive view of the entire region at the top of that lookout. The air was fresh and intoxicating.

Then there were the fires. Most of the fires were small and manageable. Others were large and scary. Most were caused by lightning strikes and a few were man-made. We used to wear special hot and heavy fire retardant suites. We carried thin metal jerry cans on our backs like knapsacks and held iron pick axes in our hands. We were dispatched from central command and followed their instructions. Sometimes we drove and trudged to fires that were easily accessible. Other times the helicopter would drop of us nearby. Some of the fires we reached during the day and others were late at night. We first assessed the situation and then made a coordinated plan to contain and put out the fire. We dug fire guards around the fire with pick axes and shovels. We fell trees and shrubs to eliminate fuel for the fire. We sprayed copious amounts of water to douse and suppress the flames. We worked hard and sweated a lot. Other times central command would call in the bombers to drop fire retardant on the fire. They would communicate with us and tell us their intentions. We would quickly move away to distance ourselves from the flames. Sometimes a bird dog or sight plane would travel overhead. Other times the bomber plane would make a pass and then return to drop its load. There was distinctive and repetitive beep-beep sound as the plane was approaching and discharging the fire retardant. It was always an exciting time.

Then there was the Carmi fire near Beaverdell. On one hot day there had been a lightning strike on the side of the mountain near the area of Carmi north of Beaverdell in the west Boundary Country towards Kelowna off Highway 33. The fire was large and growing. Water bombers, fire trucks and numerous forestry personal were dispatched to the site. Central command sent orders that our initial attack crew was to fly out immediately. They had a specific job for us to protect a house from being consumed by the fire. The helicopter dropped us off a short distance from the house. The fire was roaring all around us. The house was a large log cabin with a green corrugated roof located at a clearing near a creek. I distinctly remember standing there amid the smoke and flames of the fire. Tall pine trees all around us were burning on fire. The flames would quickly consume the tree and form a large candle flame at the top that was about the same height as the tree. The candling flame of the tree made a loud hissing and popping sound as the tree quickly burnt up. It was scary and awe inspiring to stand there in the middle of this huge fire with nothing but a jerry can filled with water and a pick axe in your hand. You quickly developed a strong and spiritual reverence of the forces of nature. Fortunately the fire did not consume the house we were assigned to protect. There was a quick change in plans at central command and they quickly removed us from this fire and flew us back to base camp in case of another emergency.

The worst thing about working as a fire fighter for the Forestry on the Initial Attack crew was being on call. As part of the job you would have to be available during peak fire season on short notice to go fire fight if needed. You were supposed to be at the forestry office located adjacent to the local airport in a quick 15 minutes time period. We didn't have cell phones and used to carry walkie-talkies that held the chatter of forestry personal communicating about work. After our regular 9 to 5 workday finished we were placed alert on call. We were paid a small pittance for being on call. It was disconcerting to be stuck at home when all your friends were having fun swimming, partying and doing other things. If you were brave and clever enough you would take your walkie-talkie and go the beach. If you were seen or caught you would get into trouble and be reprimanded. I decided to go golfing with my friends at Christina Lake when I was on call one evening. There was a fire call, I was late getting back and got a stern talking to. Another time the leader of our crew was a young forestry graduate from Selkirk College named Charlie. He was from Nakusp and he lived in room above one of the local taverns. There was a fire call late one evening. Charlie had been sitting in the tavern for most of the night and had been imbibing in more than a few libations. We picked him up and helped him make it through the rest of the night at a small fire up Santa Rosa by Christina Lake. I worked as a fire fighter for the Forestry during my summer vacation from university for three years in a row. It was the best summer job I ever had.

CHAPTER 15

The Kettle River Raft Race

Grand Forks is a small, pretty country city nestled between the mountains of the southern interior of British Columbia. It is located in a wide valley that abuts the Canadian-United States border. It is located between the sunny Okanagan desert to the west and the craggy Selkirk Mountains of the Kootenays to the east. It is called the Sunshine Valley because it gets a lot sunshine during the year and is a good place to grow vegetables and fruit. Grand Forks gets its name because two rivers merge and have their confluence there. The colder Granby River to the north meets the warmer Kettle River to south and west. The Kettle River is a 282 kilometre (175 mile) tributary of the Columbia River that snakes its way back and forth across parts of Canada and the United States. The river lazily crosses over the border at the Carson border crossing east of Grand Forks from Danville, Washington. Once back in Canada the river slowly curves and twists it way to downtown Grand Forks where it meets up with the Granby River. It then continues east to the Cascade border crossing over where once again it enters the US and turns south. The Kettle River is generally a calm, placid river that is great for swimming and tubing in the summer. However, in the spring of each year the river swells with the winter snowpack melt high up at its source in the Monashee Mountains to the North.

The Lions Club is a philanthropic and charitable organization that helps support the civic, cultural, social and moral welfare of a community. The Grand Forks Lion's Club would organize an annual raft race on the Kettle River on the Father's Day weekend in the middle of June of each year. Anybody could enter the race and paddle down the river for about four miles from old Carson Bridge to City Park located in downtown Grand Forks. At the city park there would be a festive and jovial celebration welcoming the participants as they finished at the beach. It was usually sunny and the park would be packed with people and alive with excitement. There was music booming in the background and loud voices echoing unintelligibly through speakers. The air was filled with the aroma of vendors selling fast food and souvenirs. Brightly coloured balloons and streamers lined the park boundaries like sequins on a dress. The mayor, councillors and other important brass would be on hand to be seen and heard. Local beauty queens would be at the podium to greet the winners and hand out prizes. The Lions Club Raft Race had a carnival-like atmosphere.

In the spring of every year the Kettle River would overflow and bulge over its banks with fast moving dirty water. The warm sun would melt the snowpack high in the mountains and fill the watershed below. The raft race would start at the site of the old Carson Bridge just east of Grand at the Canada-US Carson border crossing. Only some big concrete piles would remain of the bridge that was once there. A short path would lead to gravelly beach at the side of the concrete abutment on the west side of the river. The water would be flowing and swirling by with great velocity. A menagerie of cars and trucks would litter the roadway. Participants were running around unloading their rafts, oars and other equipment. Spectators were standing by on clear vantage points to get a good look at the start of the race. Lions Club members wore distinctive vests and hats and were positioned at optimal locations to direct traffic. Some executive in charge was barking orders through a hand held loud speaker trying to get things organized.

There were somewhere between 40 and 50 entrants in the Lions Club Raft Race. Each entrant would be two people with one raft. There were two categories, one for male participants and one for female participants. The race was mainly competitive, but some individuals chose to decorate their rafts like a float in a parade. Some rafts would be adorned with streamers, balloons and fake sails. Other rafts were made to look like a pirate ship or speedboat. Some of the participants decided to have fun, dress in outlandish costumes and float down the river with an icebox full of beverages. Regardless, the raft had to be constructed to specific measurements of size, shape and materials according to the rules of the race. The rafts had to be made from rubber inner tubes about the size of a truck tire. No more than three tubes were held together held by some rigging material of ropes and cords. On top of the tubes was a framework jig or template that allowed for seats. Beyond that you could be creative and ingenuous as you liked.

My friend Faron and I decided to enter the Lions Club Raft race one year. We were both 19 years old and were young and strong. Faron was a track and field athlete who was a very fast runner and hurdler. He also lifted weights to gain power and strength. I was taller and bigger than him and was pretty strong and powerful myself. My dad worked the Ministry of Highways and was able to get us some top of the line inner tubes from some of the trucks that worked out of his shop. I blew up the tubes with an air compressor in my dad's garage being careful to slightly over inflate them. I created a flat wood template that looked like a ladder for rigging. Faron came over and we put the parts of the raft together. We laid the three inner tubes in succession, placed the wood template carefully on top and tied the jig with ropes and cords. We were careful to tip the front tube slightly upward so that it would plane over the water in front of it. We put two flat squares of plywood with carpet on top of the jig that would serves as our seats. Some other entrants actually used the top part of kitchen chairs, but we thought the extra height would cause excess drag on our raft. We even experimented with putting Vaseline all over the bottom of our raft so that it would have less friction and move quickly. We worked on our raft meticulously with careful attention to detail and forethought.

We spent the better part of several days putting our raft together, breaking it down and putting it back together again. When it was finally complete we loaded the craft in the back of my dad's old baby blue GMC truck and drove to where the race would start. Faron parked his car at City Park so we could pick up the truck after completing a trial run down the river. We put on our life jackets, picked up our paddles and waded into the river. Faron got on the raft first and sat in front. I pushed us out and jumped on the rear. The current picked us up and we were off. We paddled together in unison. One, two, three, four paddles then switch sides simultaneously. We used j-strokes or paddling with a strong back stroke then arcing out slightly in the shape of a "j." We practiced back strokes the slowed our position and helped us better maneuver around some object. We analyzed the river to see where the current was fastest and tried to stick to those parts. We paid close attention to the corners where the river snaked its way towards down towards City Park. We were careful to avoid sandbars and areas of dead water that would slow us down. We watched for dead heads and log snags that poked out of the water and were careful to avoid them. After slightly more than an hour we made it to City

Park. Our shoulders ached with the exertion of paddling. We were slightly wet from the splash of the paddle hitting the water and the occasional times that we smacked our paddles on the water to soak each other. We worked hard preparing for the race and had a lot of fun. We made several more practice runs in anticipation of the race. We came very adept at reading the river and paddling efficiently.

When the day of the race came we were giddy with excitement. We loaded our raft onto my dad's truck and made our way to the Carson Crossing. We joined the other competitors standing waste deep in the water. Someone in the Lions Club shot a fake gun shell in the air to announce the start of the race and were off. We paddled hard and quickly made our way to the front of the pack. People were lining the banks of the Kettle River cheering us and the other competitors on. The river made s-shaped curves along the natural contour of the landscape as it made its way downtown. We continued to paddle with reckless abandon and unbridled enthusiasm. By the Almond Gardens Bridge one raft caught up to us and passed us, no matter how hard we paddled. The Quiring brothers were bigger, older and stronger men. They had facial hair, big biceps and legs as large as tree trunks. They were famous hockey players who played on the Grand Forks Border Bruins Hockey Team. They had won the last five Lions Club Raft Races and were the favorites to win again. By the time we made it to City Park the Quiring brothers had finished and won the race. We pulled our raft out of the water, wobbled up the sandy embankment and crossed the finish line. We came in second place, reluctantly shook the victor's hands and had fun at the rest of the festivities at the park.

The following year we decided to go in the Lions Club Raft Race again. We had licked our wounds, learned from our mistakes and were eager to make amends for our woes. Again we constructed our raft from scratch, made modifications to its design and practiced several times down the river before the race. We were now older, stronger and perhaps a little wiser. Like before there were 40 to 50 entrants in the race. The gun shot rang out in the air and the race was on. We paddled harder than the previous year and again were quickly out in the lead. The banks of the river were cluttered with spectators cheering and honking the car horns as we passed by. We paddled in steady rhythmic unison with powerful efficient strokes. We maintained our lead, looked back nervously over our shoulders and kept paddling hard. Nobody caught up to us and by the time we rounded the last stretch to City Park we were wild with excitement. At the beach there we jumped off our raft and waddled up to the finish line with weak, numb legs and sore, burning shoulders. We won the race.

A huge crowd was cheering us on at the finish line. People were screaming, whistling and clapping their hands. We dropped our raft down at the top of bank, gave each other a hug and collapsed on top of our vessel. As the other entrants crossed the finish line we cordially greeted them. The Quiring brothers came in a short time after us. We smiled coyly, shook their hands and congratulated them. We made our way to the beer gardens and food vendor area. A band was playing in the background and the distinctive smell of fried food filled the air. People in the crowd were chattering to each other like a clutch of chickens in a hen house. After a while they announced the awards ceremony and we went on stage. We collected our trophy, had our pictures taken and got hugs and kisses from Miss Grand Forks. The afternoon was warm and comfortable and the beer tasted good.

The plot thickens and boils over. That Sunday in June 1985 would ring down to me like a day in infamy. I didn't really understand the Scottish quote "oh what a tangled web we weave when we practice to deceive" until shortly after this day. Leanne was an older woman who Faron was currently dating. She was an attractive blond who worked in a local bank. She also just happened to be the ex-wife of Gerry Quiring, one of the guys we just beat in the raft race. They were apparently separated at the time and seeing other people. As it turns out, the person his ex-wife was seeing just coincidentally happened to be my friend Faron. Although cordial to each other there seemed to be some hidden innuendo and pensive animosity between Faron and Gerry. The afternoon continued unabated with robust celebration.

After the party at City Park was finishing in the early evening, we decided to continue our celebration at Faron's house in the country. Now at this time Faron had been diamond drilling with his father in northern British Columbia for a while. He made good money and bought himself a Pontiac Trans Am. It was a hot muscle car. It had a large and powerful 454 cubic inch v-8 engine with big tires and mags. It had a raised duel air intake and a spoiler in the back. It idled rhythmically with low grunts and roared when you pressed on the gas pedal. Faron, Leanne, Loresa and I jumped in the car. I sat in the passenger seat next to Faron and the girls sat in the back. We raced out of City Park and proceeded to do donuts in front the Co-op Building a short distance away. His tires squealed and rubber formed wisps of pungent smoke as he spun his wheels against the hot asphalt. The girls and I put on our seatbelts. He turned right on 72nd avenue then we sped down and turned right again on 2nd street. He accelerated down 2nd street on a bridge over the Kettle River and continued south past Ruckle Addition and an Industrial Park. Last thing I remember is that we were speeding down the street over some railway tracks and then the car just weaved off the road.

I vaguely recall lying upside in the car and hearing heavy breathing. Some paramedics pulled me out of the vehicle. I was awake but dazed. One eye was looking one way and the other eye was looking the other way. Some nice lady was holding my hand doing to reiki on me. I asked someone for a cigarette and had a light. I don't smoke, but I thought this would help me relax and figure out what happened. I went to the hospital for a checkup and was discharged a short time later. I had some scrapes and bruises and probably a concussion. I asked about the other occupants of the car. They told me everybody survived, but were injured more than I was. Loresa had stayed overnight at the hospital and had more bruises and scrapes. Leanne was kept in the hospital and had some more serious scrapes and bruises. Faron was injured more and was in a coma. He would stay in hospital for several more weeks before he was released.

After that car crash we seemed to go our separate ways. Faron moved out of town and continued to work elsewhere at different jobs. I went back to university to continue my studies after that summer ended. We grew apart and never really did talk about that day much afterwards. We only referred to it as "the accident" in past tense. When I returned home the following summer, I went in the raft race with my friend Jamie. We came in second that year and came in first the following year. After that the Lions Club held the raft race event for a few more years then cancelled it altogether. After all the excitement, buildup and letdown, the raft race was never really the same after that event. We quickly fell from grace, licked our wounds, thanked our lucky stars and moved on with life. What did I learn from that? Sometimes we make poor choices. Moments of glory are fleeting. Stupid is as stupid does. Or maybe life is precious. I don't know for certain, but we sure did have a lot of fun when I was young doing those raft races in Grand Forks on those warm, sunny Father's Day weekends in June of those years.

CHAPTER 16

Occam's Razor and Henry Thoreau

The Law of Parsimony is general law of philosophy that is also known as Occam's razor. I was first introduced to this rule in the book called "Listening to the Earth" by Robert F. Harrington. He was a retired school teacher, writer and environmentalist who lived closely with nature in the mountains near Nakusp, British Columbia. Briefly stated, the Law of Parsimony says that "entities should not be divided beyond necessity." That is, a simpler explanation to a problem is preferential to a more complicated one. Or, don't make things more complicated than they should be. Or, don't divide things more than they need to be divided. I apply the Law of Parsimony to many aspects of my life including health and nutrition.

When I was in grade 5 we had a class assembly in the gymnasium of Perley Elementary School. We were shown the movie "My Side of the Mountain" based on a book by Jean George. The movie was about a young 13 year old boy who ran away from home in the city to live in a hollowed out tree in the Catskill Mountains for a year. The movie basically chronicles his life for the year as he battled the elements living in the wilds of nature on his own and going through a cold up-state New York winter. The book and the movie was raw and unfettered. I wanted to be like the boy in the book. I wanted to run away and live in the woods for a year too.

When I was a teenager I liked to read books. I had a voracious appetite for knowledge and I enjoyed reading all types of books. In Grand Forks there was only one book store in town called the Mir Bookstore. It was operated by the affable Jim P. He let me browse in the aisles reading books for hours there. It was there that I came across the classic literary novel called Walden by Henry David Thoreau. Henry Thoreau was an 18th century author who lived New England and wrote about living in harmony with nature. He was so inspired that he left his small community in

Concord, Massachusetts and set about living in a small one room cabin on the shores of Walden Pond for over a year. He wrote the American classic best seller called "Walden" based on his experiences there. "Walden" was one of my favorite books.

Thoreau explained why he wanted to live in the woods in the following quote. He wrote, "I went to the woods because I wished to live deliberately, to front only the essential facts of life…and not, when I came to die, discover that I had not lived." It was living raw at the bone where it was sweetest. He wanted to cut out the clutter and distractions that divert attention away from what is really important in life. He basically said that people were too busy in their daily lives going about their business, family life and work. They were missing out on the most important stuff. They were missing out about understanding the true nature of reality. They were missing out about living and appreciating the present moment, ruminating about the past and worrying about the future. Simplifying one's life and communing with nature were the easiest ways to front the essential facts of life and live deliberately.

At the Mir Bookstore, I also came across a magazine called Common Sense written by Robert F. Harrington. It was a magazine that expounded the virtues of living simply in harmony with Mother Nature. He was heavy into the philosophy of Thoreau, Emerson and Lin Yutang. He talked about recycling, wood stoves and growing your own garden. I resonated with a lot of his ideas. He also wrote several books including my favorite called "Thoughts from the Woods." He lived in Galena Bay near Nakusp, British Columbia and appeared to be living in harmony with nature. "Thoughts from the Woods" was a book a short stories and musings of his adventures and thoughts about living in the wilds. He talked about the birds and other wildlife he saw there, going for a walk on winter's day, looking in awe at the nights sky or simply relaxing by his wood stove as it crackled away. It was a relaxing, meditative book

Later in life when I was living and working in Kelowna I corresponded with Mr. Harrington and we became friends. We shared some conversations, bartered some natural supplements for his books and exchanged some correspondence. I appreciated his wit and wisdom and sensible approach to life. One day I thought I might live like Henry Thoreau or R.F. Harrington. Regardless, their philosophy and ideas have influenced me and inspired me. I love hiking in the outdoors and imbuing that natural beauty all around me. I feel relaxed and invigorated when I am outside breathing fresh air and reflecting on the incredible and awesome universe all around us. There is something beckoning in the nature world that I have a deep, heartfelt appreciation of nature and reverence of life. It calls out to me and somehow the vastness and stillness resonates with my soul.

The Law of Parsimony exemplifies an approach to dealing with life and the natural world around us. It tells to not divide things beyond necessity. Keep things simple. The simplest answer is often the best. Don't make things more complicated than the need to be. The world is already too complicated with work, life, computers, emails, the internet, radio, television and cell phones. There are too many distractions, encumbrances and diversions. We should simplify and focus on what is essentially important. I learned that the law of parsimony applies to areas of diet and nutrition, with specific emphasis on juicing. See what you think.

Juicing is an extraction procedure that uses a mechanical device to separate the liquid portion of a fruit or vegetable from the pulp of fiber. Juicing is believed to concentrate the enzymes, vitamins and minerals and phyto-nutrients from the less desirable and less useful pulp. While this may be true the pulp and fiber is still important and useful in human nutrition. Juicing is believed to be a useful and practical tool for health and healing.

Many ad hoc nutritionists advocate using a specific juicer to extract and concentrate potent nutrients. When I was in naturopathic school at Bastyr College in the late 1980's in Seattle, Washington, I had the good fortune to have Dr. Michael Murray as an inspiring teacher and mentor. Dr. Murray gave me his Champion juicer when I was helping him move from his home in Bellevue. While there are many other brands of machines, the Champion juicer is often considered to be the Cadillac of juicers. I see new models of this juicer for sale at stores like Costco for several hundred dollars. I have kept this juicer for all these years, although I must confess that I hardly use it now.

While I was at Bastyr College, I had the good fortune of meeting the famous nutritionist, author and physician Dr. Bernard Jensen. I attended one of his talks at a theatre hall at the University of Washington. He was an old time natural healer who advocated healthy diet and good nutrition. He wrote more than 50 books and operated a successful healing sanitarium in Escondido, California. He travelled extensively and studied the diet and nutrition of many people and cultures throughout the world. I remember asking him a question at the end of his lecture about what was the most important thing about diet and nutrition. In my youthful exuberance I was expecting a long, complicated scientific answer to my question. He thought about the question carefully with his grey hair ruffled and his bright eyes twinkling. He replied that the most important thing about all these diets is to just simply eat healthy. He said, "Eat at least 5 or 6 vegetables per day, 2 or 3 fruits, some whole grain or cereals, nuts and seeds and a little bit of healthy protein." I thanked him for his answer and smiled.

I like to make my health drink for breakfast in the warm summer months. I put one whole carrot, one stalk of celery, a few sprigs of broccoli, a handful of kale or spinach, one banana and one half cup of frozen blueberries. I pour some soy milk, almond milk, rice milk or coconut milk and add some water. I sometimes add an avocado or plain protein powder. I will often add a few tablespoons of peanut butter or almond butter. I puree the mixture in my blender. I used to have an Osterizer blender but that broke after a lot of use and now I use a stainless steel Cuisinart blender. The frozen blueberries turn the blend a dark purple colour with the texture of a cool milkshake. Like most men, to use the cliché, I drink my concoction directly from the glass blender carafe for breakfast.

Whatever nutritional philosophical bent you prescribe to, juicing or not, keep it simple. It is far more important to eat a variety of fruits and vegetables, organic or not, with the more colour the better. Every morning when I make my health shake I try to use plenty of vegetables and fruits. It tastes good, it has a lot of fruit and vegetables and I think it is a healthy way to start the day, fiber and all. I don't use an expensive juice extractor, but use a simple blender. I used to use green powder blends with 30 or 40 different fruits, vegetables and herbs, but I found a lot of them had too much ingredients and some of them bothered me. I like the simplicity of mixing what fruits and vegetables I like and that taste good together. When I drink my health beverage for breakfast, I often smile and think about the Law of Parsimony with regards to diet and nutrition and the wisdom of Bernard Jensen.

You can apply the Law of Parsimony and the wisdom of Henry Thoreau to your personal life with good results. Thoreau once said, "Our

119

life is frittered away by detail. An honest man has hardly need to count more than his ten fingers, or in extreme cases he may add his ten toes, and lump the rest. Simplicity, simplicity, simplicity! I say, let your affairs be as two or three, and not a hundred or a thousand; instead of a million count half a dozen, and keep your accounts on your thumb nail. In the midst of this chopping sea of civilized life, such are the clouds and storms and quick sands and thousand-and-one items to be allowed for, that a man has to live, if he would not founder and go to the bottom and not make his port at all, by dead reckoning, and he must be a great calculator indeed who succeeds. Simplify, simplify. Instead of three meals a day, if it be necessary eat but one; instead of a hundred dishes, five; and reduce other things in proportion."

CHAPTER 17

The Legend of the Komodo Dragon

Everybody likes a good story. Storytelling is an art as ancient as the times. It involves the verbal or written telling of story using words, images and sounds. It often involves the use of embellishment and improvisation. It often is rich in is metaphors and similes. Vibrant storytelling is engaging, inspiring and uplifting. It can be used for education, entertainment and cultural engagement. It often has a meaning and can instill moral values. Storytelling blends and weaves a narrative. It encourages the imagination and visual imagery. Storytelling is an art form that is fun and exciting to hear.

My Uncle Mike was a talker. He had the gift of gab. He was a frequent and requested speaker at wedding, funerals and meetings. He could tell a story that would keep your attention for hours. I remember Mike had this friend named Bill who he met at AA or Alcoholics Anonymous meeting. Bill was trying to explain the game of baseball to some foreign visitors. He was explaining what the bat catcher did. He was having trouble communicating to his friends. His friends couldn't understand him. Mike interjected. He started explaining what the bat catcher did. Mike was waving his arms with an imaginary glove and baseball. He was bending down on his knees rocking up and down and gesticulating to an imaginary batter and pitcher. He explained with an undulating vocal tone while he was smacking his imaginary glove. His use of visual imagery was impeccable. In your mind's eye you were right there at the ball game. The foreign visitors were laughing and rolling their eyes. They knew exactly what a bat catcher did.

I tried to emulate my Uncle Mike when I was telling a story. When one of my daughters was in a high school English class, one of her assignments was to write a pourquoi story. According to Wikipedia, a pourquoi story is a story of why something the way it is. It is also known as an origin story of meaning and answers. It is a fictional narrative that explains the why about some phenomenon. For example, why a snake has no legs, or why a tiger has stripes. Many legends and folk tales are pourquoi stories. Here is my pourquoi story that I told to my children when they were young. I wrote it from a third person perspective of my daughter who is narrating the story. Here it goes.

Nobody knows why there are no mosquitoes in Kelowna? Some people say it's because of pesticides sprayed on orchards. Other people say its to do with all the black birds eating mosquitoes. My dad told me it was due to the Komodo dragon living up somewhere in the North Glenmore highlands above our home.

Legend has it that there is a large, ferocious Komodo dragon running wild in the mountains of North Glenmore in Kelowna. I know this is true because my dad told me so when I was young. I was ten years old when I learnt that the Komodo dragon existed. My dad told my sister and me that some young boy in North Glenmore got a small lizard as a pet. He kept the small lizard in a shoe box with air holes in his bedroom. The lizard was really hungry so it ate a lot of crickets and grasshoppers. It kept on growing bigger and bigger. One day the boy and his family decided they couldn't keep it any longer. So one day the boy and his family took the lizard and released him into the forested mountains of North Glenmore. And the legend of the Komodo dragon was born.

Komodo dragons are large lizards native to Indonesia Island of southern Asia. The Komodo dragon grows up to 3 meters or 10 feet in length from their nose to the tip of their tale. They can weigh up to 70 kilograms or 150 pounds. They have a long, yellow forked tongue that can smell things and large, sharp claws on its feet. They have up to sixty sharp teeth, have one ear and can live up to 30 years old. They can see up to 1000 meters away during the day and can be blind at night. They can run up to 20 kilometers per hour and like to hunt in the afternoon. Komodo dragons dig holes in the ground for shelter and stay in the shade when it is hot. They like to eat small animals, birds and mammals. They are shy creatures that flee at the sight of humans. They make strange hissing sounds and can pound the ground with their feet. There are believed to be only 4000 to 5000 Komodo dragons left in the world.

The Legend of the Komodo Dragon

The way my dad told it, there was one large, ferocious Komodo dragon eating and living well in the North Glenmore highlands just above our home. We were told to be careful and on guard at all times when where hiking in the mountains there. My dad said that was why there were no mosquitoes in summer time around Kelowna. He drew some sort of food web explain his theory. He said that Komodo dragons were carnivorous and liked to eat small animals, birds and mammals. Frogs eat mosquitoes. And birds, beavers, skunks, black birds, snakes, porcupines and raccoons eat frogs. Well there were a lot of frogs in the ponds and lakes in the North Glenmore highlands. There were very few beavers, skunks, black birds, snakes, porcupines and raccoons. The Komodo dragon ate the beavers, skunks, snakes, porcupines and raccoons. There were no predators trying to eat the frogs and the frog population exploded. The millions of frogs ate all the mosquitoes. And this was why the Komodo dragon was responsible for there being no mosquitoes in Kelowna during the summer time.

My cousin Sasha was a redneck, country boy from Grand Forks. He was obnoxious and annoying. He had an enormous appetite and liked to eat everything in sight. He liked baseball, fishing and snowmobiling in winter. His friends were Curtis and Joey. He liked to play jokes and pranks. Once he told Curtis that he found a whole bunch of gum balls that they were really colored paintballs. He gave some to Curtis. Curtis ate them and he was sick for week afterwards. Sasha liked watching Duck Dynasty and Family Guy. His two favorite sayings were "I don't know" and "whatever." He was a little eccentric, immature and liked to get his way all the time. He was a mama's boy and his goal was to live in parent's basement for the rest of his life. He was a cheapskate and he made me search on the ground for spare change for an hour so he could buy a candy bar for himself. He liked to tease everybody, especially my grandmother Nellie. He knows my Baba hates to have the window open with cold wind blowing on her ears. On a recent shopping trip to Colville he left his window open all the way home just to tease her. When they later went for lunch he made swamp water for Baba who thought it was just regular Dr. Pepper. He added extra salt and vinegar. She was sick all the way home. My cousin Sasha was a 15 year old trouble maker.

Sasha's younger sister was Mary. She was smarter than he was, liked school and wanted to go away to university when she was older. She had a nice personality and reminded me of a puppy. She was always seemed friendly and nice and never said anything mean or bad. She worked in a busy restaurant and the only thing I remember was her pony tail bouncing up and down as she raced from table to table serving customers. My cousins Sasha and Mary used to come over in summertime to visit us.

I remember one summer my cousin Sasha and Mary came to visit us in Kelowna one day. Sasha was in his usual awful, cantankerous mood. He locked Mary, my sister and me out of our house and made us use a steep ladder to crawl back inside. He got us to shoot hard hockey pucks at my parent's garage door. He told us girls had weak hockey shots and he wanted to help us improve them. Boy was my mom and dad mad when they saw the garage door. My parents gave us badminton rackets to go play outside on the front lawn. Sasha broke all our badminton rackets because he was trying to hit the bees that were attacking him outside. My dad told him the story of the Komodo dragon as a way of distracting him before he destroyed our house. He got really excited. My dad told us we would go on a field trip the next day in search of the Komodo dragon. We started to get ready by gathering supplies for the expedition. Sasha got a butterfly net to put over the head of the Komodo dragon. He also got rope to make a trap for dragon's leg. We got a bag of marshmallows to use as bait to help capture the giant reptile.

We set off the next morning after breakfast in search of the Komodo dragon of the North Glenmore highlands. We walked on a path up the mountains through the forest of pine trees, Oregon grape root, arrow leaf balsam flowers and snow berry bushes. We were excited and nervous. We jumped up with every rustle in a bush, chirp of a bird or quack of a duck. We checked under logs, behind bushes and around trees. We came to a small lake called Still Pond. It was alive with activity and noise. Mallard ducks and black coots swam in the water. Grasshoppers and crickets chirped away. Red winged black birds whistled and Canadian geese honked away. The pond was surrounded by bulrushes and poison ivy. The water was rich in algae and weeds. It had strong stench. The sun was hot and golden.

We walked around Still Pond looking for the Komodo dragon but couldn't find it. We got bored and tired. Sasha got really excited when he saw turtles along the shore of the pond clinging to logs and rocks. Their head and shelled bodies stuck out of the water in the sun. He decided he was going to capture a turtle and keep it as a pet. He took the butterfly net and stepped carefully through the bulrushes on logs and rocks. He crept up slowly but as soon as the turtles heard or saw him they took off under the water. He tried this procedure many times. Just as he was getting close to the turtles they would snap and disappear. During his last attempt he slipped and fell in the dirty, smelly water. We all laughed and roared unsympathetically. He was covered in dark goop that smelled like bad fish. Boy was he mad. He wouldn't talk to us all the way back home. My dad felt bad and took us all to McDonald's for lunch. My cousin Sasha ate three Big Mac's and one big ice cream cone.

We never did find or see the Komodo dragon. Now that I am older, I don't even know if there was a Komodo dragon in the North Glenmore highlands. All I know is that my cousin Sasha was a rambunctious trouble maker but he was kind of fun to be around. We had a lot of laughs and good adventures with him. I still don't know why there are no mosquitoes in Kelowna to this day. Oh yeh, the only lizard that we ever saw in North Glenmore was a small, green Gecko. It was only about three inches long and we were all too scared to pick it up, except for Sasha. The end.

CHAPTER 18
John Bastyr, Seattle and UW

I graduated from Grand Forks Secondary School in 1983. I went to Selkirk College in Castlegar for one year. I transferred over to the University of British Columbia in 1984. I studied sciences, mainly biology and chemistry. At the time I didn't realize it, but UBC was like a prim and proper Ivy League school. I still enjoyed it and had a lot of fun there. I graduated from UBC in 1987 with a Bachelor of Science degree in zoology. I applied and was accepted to study Naturopathic Medicine at Bastyr College of Naturopathic Medicine in Seattle, Washington in 1987. This private college was named after the pioneer Naturopathic doctor named John Bastyr. I didn't know much about the college and was limited to only what I read about in the brochures I received. After graduating from university I wanted to further my studies and get a suitable vocation. I liked science and dealing with people and I thought I might want to become a doctor.

I grew up in the small, rural town of Grand Forks in the southern interior British Columbia. My mother was of Russian Doukhobor ancestry and my father was of Polish and Belorussia descent. My parents only rarely went to doctors and seldom took prescription drugs. Our family had a big garden and ate mainly organic food long before it was fashionable to eat organic. I liked studying sciences in school and thought I might pursue a scientific career after I graduated from high school. When I was fifteen years old I heard a group of doctors speak at the Dom or Russian Community building in our town. They were a group of naturopathic doctors who were cycling around North America and speaking about the virtues of good health and nutrition. Closely aligned to the principles of the Doukhobor religion, they espoused the ideas of eating healthy, taking vitamins and taking responsibility for your health. I thought the talk was fascinating and it planted a seed in my brain.

My family used to go on shopping trips to Kelowna when I was young. Kelowna was the beautiful, larger city on Okanagan Lake that was famous for orchards and fruit. Orchard Park Mall was the largest shopping mall between Vancouver and Calgary. Dr. Craig Wagstaff was a Naturopathic doctor who had his office right across from the mall. I used to visit him there periodically and he showed me how he practiced. It was inspiring and intriguing. He had a busy practice and he used natural medicines, like vitamins, minerals, herbs and botanical medicines to treat disease and illness. He showed me his practice, let me observe how he diagnosed and treated patients and let me inspect his pharmacy of natural remedies. After watching him for a while, I decided I wanted to be a Naturopathic doctor.

In the fall of 1987, I enrolled in Bastyr College and moved to Seattle, Washington. It was exciting, as I was moving to different country to study. I loaded up all my possessions in my black GMC Blazer and drove across the border to Seattle. A school administrator at the college invited me to live in her basement suite when I first moved there. I discovered that the school itself was a renovated elementary school near the University of Washington near 45th street and the I-5 freeway. It was a small three story brick building. It was earthy, quaint and friendly. They had a section of mail boxes for all the students on the second floor. The blackboards were a little low, the classrooms a slightly small, but the people were friendly and nice. The Naturopathic program was a four year post-graduate degree program that closely resembled a traditional medical school. It diverged for mainstream medicine in terms of therapeutics and treatments. They were about forty students per class. I was one of the youngest in my class. I was 22 years old and was full of youthful exuberance.

First year at Bastyr College included courses in anatomy, biochemistry, physiology and other basic life sciences. Some of it was review and some of it was new. I loved the sciences and generally enjoyed all my classes at the school. I found it very fascinating and intriguing to learn about the human body. My favorite class in my first year at school was anatomy. We had anatomy lectures on campus and dissection class in a small lab on the Ave near the University of Washington. The Ave was the slang term used to describe the major commercial and retail street next the University of Washington. It was over eight blocks long and was full of all sorts of food vendors and funky retail shops. The lab was located in the back of a bank building at the corner of a major intersection on the Ave. The windows were frosted over so you couldn't look in and couldn't look out. Unbeknown to the thousands of students who walked by outside, this little indiscrete lab contained five of six cadavers that were used for dissection. While people were walking by outside, we were dissecting these bodies inside. It was fascinating to look at the real anatomical structure of the text books we studied. I remember we tried to determine why these people passed away. I distinctly remember looking at the lungs of one of the cadavers. Normally the lungs were large, pink spongy sacs. This cadaver had black, shrivelled lungs. This person was probably a smoker and died of lung cancer. I was excited to be first year Naturopathic medical student.

Class lectures were held at the elementary school campus. Labs in cell biology and histology were held at Seattle Community College towards the downtown of the city. They had good quality microscopes that we used to study cell structure. I discovered REI when I used to go to this lab class. It was a large, world class outdoor store called Recreation Equipment Incorporated. It was a cooperative that sold quality outdoor gear, camping equipment and clothing. It fueled my interest to explore the mountains around the Pacific Northwest while attending school.

Seattle was a large, beautiful city located on the shores of Puget Sound and the Cascade mountains. It was full of evergreen trees and had lot of parkland. The iconic Mount Rainier rises to the south east of Seattle and is clearly visible for hundreds of miles on a clear day. This rounded mountain is the tallest mountain in the Cascade Range and is still an active volcano. During my stay in Seattle I was able to go climbing and hiking on Mount Rainier. It is an incredible and surreal experience. I learned technical skills of mountaineering and climbing. I was also able to climb Mount Adams in southern Washington and Mount Baker just south of Vancouver. I remember we spent two days climbing Mount Baker early one summer. The leader of the group was the middle-age principal of a private Catholic school in Kelowna named Father Bob. We camped above the cloud line at over 8000 feet. In the early morning we set out to summit the peak. We were roped up, wore crampons and gained our balance with the help of an ice axe. We weaved upwards through a crevassed glacier. My friend in the group was a young lady named Liza from New Denver. She was an incredibly strong and powerful climber. My other friend Kim and I let her carry the heaviest pack up to the summit. I was tired and not really proud of this fact, but I didn't let my male pride dissuade me. I also forgot my sunglasses at base camp. We made it to the summit by lunch time. You could smell sulphur gas ebbing from this active volcanic mountain. After a short stay we headed back down the mountain. I was euphoric and fatigued at the same time. I developed snow blindness and my eyes were really sore for a week afterwards. Overall climbing Mount Baker and the other peaks was an incredible and uplifting experience.

I was shocked to discover that there were only four to five ice rinks in all of Seattle. I came from Vancouver which had numerous rinks dispersed throughout the city. Drop in hockey in Seattle was exorbitantly expensive. I decided not to play hockey my first year in Seattle. In the fall of my first year there I decided to join a ski instructor club called Webb Ski. This volunteer group would meet at the top of Snoqualmie Summit on Interstate-90 between Seattle and Spokane on weekends. There was three small ski mountains connected together including Ski Acres and Alpental. I would instruct young children and teenagers how to ski. We got a free ski pass and a bright red ski jacket. It was a lot of fun there and I went skiing almost every weekend in the winter of my first year in Seattle.

I went hiking to the Grand Canyon in Arizona with a friend I met at the Webb Ski School. We travelled to Phoenix, Arizona, rented a car and travelled five hours north to Flagstaff and then to the Grand Canyon. My first impression of the viewing the Grand Canyon was incredible. I was awestruck at its magnitude, size and beauty. You felt like a small pebble in a huge universe. The canyon is over mile wide and at least a mile deep. It had layers of different coloured sedimentary rock stacked on top of each other. You almost felt as if you could look back through the aeons of time as you stared out across the canyon. You could sit on your lawn chair looking at the reflection of the sun on the canyon for hours. Nothing changed except for the different colours of reflected light off the rock walls lining the canyon. We went hiking from the south rim to the bottom of the canyon to the Colorado River. It was a desert and it was very hot there. There was a lot of cacti dotting the landscape. It was a good thing we had lots of water to drink. Experiencing the Grand Canyon was an awesome hiking adventure.

In my second year of school at Bastyr College, I moved out of the basement I was living at and moved in with my friend Susan. She was a student in my class. She was older and she was a very good skier. She

Uncle Mickey the Barber
lived in a house with two other people closer to the college on 85th street. The owner of the house was a Vietnam veteran named Denny, who wasn't around that much. The other resident was a school teacher named Cathy. We each had a room and shared a bathroom and a kitchen. We all got along and our living relationship worked out well for the most part. The best part of living there was the cedar hot tub in the back yard.

My landlord and housemate Denny made a rustic cedar hot tub with a pop up lid and cedar deck in the corner of the yard. The hot tub was warm and relaxing. During the cold winter months the hot tub was inviting and invigorating. In the evening after a hard day at school you would go jump in and unwind. After playing hockey, skiing or some other athletic endeavor you would soak and mend your aching body. I particularly remember the fog around the tub. Of course it rains a lot in a coastal city like Seattle. The cold rain and mist would meet the warmer hot tub air and create an earie fog all around the backyard. The porch light in the back would reflect through the fog and create and a ghostly back drop. I would spend many hours in the tub relaxing, reflecting and thinking. Other times the tub would be the centre of socialization and entertainment. Having that hot tub was a nice little perk.

Second year at naturopathic school was more challenging. We had more interesting courses in microbiology, neuroanatomy and pathology. My favorite course in second year was pharmacology and pharmacognosy. I enjoyed learning about the chemistry of drugs and plants. We had many courses and it was a lot of information to absorb. We had some inspiring teachers and I was motivated to learn. One of my favorite teachers there was a naturopathic doctor named Jane. Many of the older students had trouble with the amount of work presented. I was young, had a pretty good brain, enjoyed learning new things and really soaked things up. I really being a student at Bastyr College.

I was exploring and getting used to Seattle. I discovered an earthy and funky bakery between Bastyr College and Green Lake. Honey Bear Bakery served homemade scones, muffins, cinnamon buns and delicious coffee. It was a popular coffee shop and bakery before Starbucks had become popular. It was a favorite student hangout to study, drink coffee or tea and have lunch. It had a big bear statue out front alerting to its name. It was kind of a hippy place with down-to-earth, organic people who didn't wear makeup and liked to talk about politics. It catered to the free-spirited, non-conformist Bohemian crowd of Seattle. Men wore their hair back in tight pony tails and women wore no makeup, earthy dresses and sandals. I enjoyed going to the Honey Bear Bakery, having a beverage and a snack and studying for hours.

Green Lake was located just down the street from Honey Bear Bakery. It was a small, pretty lake with a park, tennis courts and a sidewalk that went around the perimetre of the lake. It was a busy area with a lot of people and plenty of ducks. I used to hang out at Green Lake. It was fun to jog around the circumference of the lake or just walk with friends. I used to play tennis there and purchased a pair of roller blades at a shop located there. There was also a soccer field there where we used to play co-ed soccer. Some of the soccer games were very competitive. I soon discovered that it was the women who were the most mean and competitive. Some of the females wouldn't think twice about kicking you in the shins if they couldn't get the ball. I enjoyed hanging out at Green Lake.

I missed playing hockey. A friend told me about the University of Washington Huskies hockey team. I decided to see if I could play for them as a walk on. I talked to the coach named Geoff, explained my situation and practiced with them. I was Canadian, I could skate and play hockey pretty well. He liked me and let me play for the team. He didn't ask questions and he was ok with the fact that I didn't go to the University of Washington. I told the other players that I was a medical student, but I think most of them knew I was a foreign student studying at Bastyr College. We practiced at the Highland Ice Rink in North Seattle. We played other teams throughout the Pacific Northwest including junior B teams in Seattle and Vancouver, Gonzaga University in Spokane and Royal Roads Military College in Victoria. It was a lot of fun and I enjoyed the camaraderie with the other players on the UW hockey team.

I had the peculiar habit of not wearing shoulder pads when I played hockey. I was still playing contact and checking was part of the game. I thought that shoulder pads would slow me down and inhibit my ability to take a good shot. I remember we were playing a junior B team in Mountlake Terrace. They were young, fast and like the physical play. One bigger player hit me from behind and on the right side. I felt pain and discovered my right clavicle was dislocated. The trainer on our team was a cute young brunette UW student from Spokane. She was what we players called a puck bunny. She liked hockey and being around hockey players. Some of the players on our team went out to a night club in downtown Seattle after the game. I was in pain and Colleen attended to me. We ended going out for a while till she dumped me at a hockey tournament in Wenatchee for an old boyfriend who happened to be another player on the team. I still really enjoyed playing hockey for the University of Washington Huskies.

In the third year of my studies at Bastyr College, courses switched from basic life sciences to diagnosis, therapeutics and treatment. The first two years of naturopathic school are almost identical to the basic training at most medical colleges. You still have to know the basics about anatomy, biochemistry and physiology. The training differs mainly in terms of therapy and treatment. Instead of recommending drugs and doing surgery all the time, you try to prescribe more natural therapies including diet, vitamins, botanical and herbs, physical medicine and acupuncture. You try to help the body and mind to heal itself. You try to stimulate the inherent healing power of nature.

The College had a clinic just off the Ave in the University District. As part of your practical training you had to do clinical work there. You would rotate working seeing patients, working in the lab and pharmacy and in the physio and manual therapy clinic there. At first it was daunting to see real live patients. You would follow a strict protocol of interviewing a patient. You would first ask subjective information pertaining to symptoms. Then you would ask and perform objective tests and gather information. Based on your findings you would formulate an assessment and treatment plan. I remember the first time I drew blood on a patient in the lab there. I middle aged male came in for tests and disclosed he was HIV positive. I had no real concept of what that meant. I was nervous and my hands were shaking, but I was still able to draw the blood. I wasn't practicing on oranges anymore, this was real life. My style developed as my confidence grew.

One of my mentors at the school was a teacher named Dr. Michael Murray. He was intelligent, young and confident. He was one of the first scientific researchers on the validation of Naturopathic medicine. He researched articles, collected data and referenced material. He wrote in magazines and published books. He developed a successful line of natural products for a popular company. He was their spokesperson who gave talks and lectures throughout the United States. He was sharp, well dressed and brash. He wore preppy clothes and kept his hair short and well groomed. He was unlike most of the other teachers and Naturopathic

132

doctors, who more resembled beatniks and hippies. Some people didn't like him, accusing him of being too commercial and scientific. Other people were jealous of him because he was rich and successful. I liked him and aspired to be like Mike.

There was a potpourri of different students from different backgrounds from all around the world at Bastyr College. There were more females than males, because I think most women are generally more conscious of their health than males. There was Leo the Rastafarian, Brian the homeopath, Peter the New England preppy and Julien the hapless romantic. There was Kay the runner, Susan the skier, Roseanne the debutante and Johanna the environmentalist. There was a mishmash of different religions, political ideals and sexual persuasions. You learned to be tolerant and were forced to communicate effectively. I didn't always agree with everybody there, but at least I would listen them out. You learned to appreciate different opinions and would come to the conclusion that there was more than one way to do something. Many times after class or lab, a group of us students would go out for appetizers and beverages at a local tavern.

During fourth year of my studies at Bastyr College I was taking specialized courses in different areas of medicine like cardiology, geriatrics, oncology and urology. It was now more practical, hands on and real. You practiced looking in ears, mouths and taking a lot of blood pressures. You discovered what areas of medicine that interested you and others that did not. I was doing more clinical work seeing patients at the school outpatient facility. I was also volunteering as a preceptor and had the opportunity to visit other practicing doctors and clinics throughout the city. I preceptored with an Osteopathic doctor named Dr. Patchen at a walk-in clinic in North Seattle. We saw all sorts of things there and even did some minor surgery. I worked with Dr. Bakken in a pain clinic in Redmond doing trigger point shots. I also followed a practical, wise old cardiologist named Dr. Gillis as he did stress tests in his office and counselled heart attack patients. Most of it was interesting. I felt more comfortable on my pathway to become a doctor and a healer.

By this time I had developed a close network of friends who were roughly the same age as I. We hung out together, roomed together at different times and studied together. We shared many enduring memories. We were poor students. We did our best to get by. Many of behaviors were determined by our student mentality and desire to have fun. We were adaptable and malleable. We were an incongruous group of misfits with different strengths and weakness who had some odd and quirky habits. In our ragtag group of friends there was Gaetano, Kim, Jonathan, Eugene and myself.

Gaetano or Gus for short was a suave Italian from Vancouver. Like myself he was Canadian and from Vancouver. He also had went to the University of British Columbia. He said he even went to medical school at UBC but dropped out for some reason and ended up at Bastyr College. He had slicked back jet black hair and wore expensive Italian clothes and shoes. I didn't know he even went to school during my first year at the naturopathic college. He stayed up late and slept in a lot. He missed a lot of his morning classes and I seldom saw him around the school. He lived with Eugene in a house with others near the University of Washington. He taught me how to make delicious Italian eggs. He had a hot black Camaro. We used to make weekend trips back to Vancouver together. He lived with his parents in Burnaby. His parents appeared to be a traditional happy family. His mother just doted on him. I remember she would come out crying when we were leaving back to Seattle. She brought his freshly pressed clothes on hangers and gave us delicious food like eggplant parmesan. Gaetano was a lady's man. He liked girls and they liked him. He had a lot of girlfriends. He dated some real attractive models. He appeared to be confident and sure of himself. He had many women phoning him from all over. They would come up to him, smile, laugh and talk to him. They would give him their numbers. He would seem nice and cordial, but also seem somewhat disinterested. He told me several times that you could always get another girlfriend, but you could never get a new mother. That seemed to be true.

Then there was Kim. He was also from Vancouver. He was pretty smart and athletic. We used to play soccer together and go hiking. He wasn't born with a silver spoon in his mouth. He was more of a hustler. He used to buy and sell things to make money. He had bought a house in the Langley from an elderly lady without putting much money down. He hung on to the house for a while and then flipped to a real estate investor for a tidy profit. His nickname was Crash because he also liked to sleep a lot and missed his morning classes. He and his dad were junk collectors and they frequented flea markets and garage sales. They reminded me of the comedy show called Sanford and Son. He also had his sure of lady friends. I remember one time we were travelling back together to

Vancouver for the weekend. Kim had this big one ton truck loaded with all sorts of used junk. It had a blue tarp around the rear box in the back tied down with rope. It was flapping around wildly in the wind as we were driving down the I-5 freeway. The cab of the truck was littered with textbooks, food containers and pop cans. Kim had a long, scruffy unshaven beard and was wearing dark sunglasses. When we came to the Canadian border the guards gave us a weird look and let us through. When we came back to the US border I had an uneasy feeling stirring in my stomach. From the long lineup we were singled out for a check and interrogation. The American border guards inspected the truck with lights, mirrors and dogs. We were taken inside the building and placed in separate rooms. Two guards approached and asked a whole bunch of questions. I showed them my student visa. Then they decided to a physical body search and I can tell you that wasn't fun. After over two hours at the border crossing they thanked us and let us go.

Jonathan and Eugene were two hapless American friends who were part of our clique. Both them were in the class one year ahead of me. Jonathan was from Connecticut with short blond hair. He reminded me of a preppy school boy from the east coast. He seemed pretty well to do, had a car and a nice apartment. He lived with his African American girlfriend Monica. She seemed nice and Jonathan and I used to play tennis together. Eugene was also from the east coast and he had a distinctive New York accent. He was a tall, slightly potbellied Italian guy with short dark hair and a groomed tight beard. He loved reggae and used to run a radio show dedicated to the music and the Rastafarian movement. Eugene used to live with Gaetano. They would laugh at each other's mannerisms and would tease each other incessantly. We would hang out together and look for trouble and other things to do.

Stella's was an Italian trattoria restaurant located in the University district a few blocks away from the Ave. Gaetano, Kim, Jonathan, Eugene and I used to frequent this establishment. It was one of our favorite hangouts and watering holes after a hard day in school. We would show up there at odd hours to eat, drink or just do nothing. Lunch was usually after 2 pm and supper was usually after 9 or 10 pm in the evening. We would try to engage and flirt with the waitresses there. Meg was a waitress who was also a student at Bastyr College. She would humour us as we teased her. We were generous with our smiles and short on out tips with her and the other waitresses. We used to sit at our favorite booth, talk about our day at school and natter about girls and other things. We would tell jokes and laugh a lot. A lot of times we did nothing there. We still had a lot of fun hanging out at Stella's. The food wasn't that bad there either.

In June of 1991, I graduated from Bastyr College after four years of study with a doctorate degree in Naturopathic Medicine. There was a small graduation ceremony at a regal setting in downtown Seattle. My parents, other family members and my girlfriend Natalie came to the event. I wore a cap and gown and received my diploma and shook hands with president of the college named Joe Pizzorno. We went out for a nice dinner after the ceremony. A few days later I packed up my stuff in my GMC Blazer and headed out of town. I drove north back to Vancouver and Canada. My experience and education at Bastyr College, Seattle and the University of Washington was wonderful. I learned lots, tried different things and generally had a lot of fun there. It was an important and distinctive part of my education. I moved back to Vancouver and then to Kelowna to practice Naturopathic Medicine and to get on with my life.

Postscript

There you have it. There is my life story so far. These were some of the more significant defining moments in the first half of my life. I hope you enjoyed them and found them entertaining. I hope even learned something from them.

I always thought that I would be writing my memoirs on a beach somewhere in Mexico. I imagined myself sitting on a chair in front of the ocean in the sun with my laptop and a margarita. It didn't quite turn out like that. Instead I wrote my memoirs in my cool basement sitting on a big fabric recliner my mother bought for me. Sometimes I had a glass of wine and the air conditioner nearby was churning away. The writing flowed easy. I suppose it was because I had something to say and I knew mostly what I was writing about. I thought it would be a relatively short book, but as I was writing I realized I had a lot more to say. I think the writing turned out ok.

I met my future wife Natalie in Grand Forks at the Yale Hotel one evening when I was home one summer from university. She was the older sister of my sister's good friend Theresa. I knew of her, but really didn't know her. My friend Jamie and I were going to the Yale Hotel Pub early one Saturday night to socialize and shoot pool. On the way in the tavern we noticed that there was a wedding next door in the Yale Hotel Restaurant. We both peaked inside and looked around. My sister's friend Theresa was getting married to an older young man named Cecil. It was nice and bright and we knew a lot of the people there. We thought what the heck and decided to go inside and join the celebration. We were dressed nicely and fit right in. There was a lot of good food, free drinks and the atmosphere was festive and joyful. We stayed there for most of the night. I had a great time. We were seated at a table with people we knew. I talked and socialized with many people. Natalie was one of the bridesmaids in the wedding party. She was busy running around greeting everybody and posing for pictures. She looked beautiful and stunning in her peach chiffon dress and dark blond hair. I chatted with her for a long time about school, work, life and other things. Later that night after the lights dimmed, the music was turned on and the dancing began. I had the good fortune of dancing with Natalie for several dances that evening. We laughed, smiled and chatted to each other in reckless oblivion. I was especially happy and content. A seed of possibilities was cast.

I have been blessed with two beautiful daughters named Rachel and Jessica. I, along with my wife Natalie, have spent a lot of time raising them. Like most parents, we made many lunches, washed a lot of clothes, drove them to school, to piano recitals and soccer practices. Now they are older and are out of their teens. I wanted to leave them something special to remember me by. I wanted to leave them something personal that revealed to them who I was and where I came from. I decided to leave them the stories of my earlier life.

We shared many special, private moments together. We would watch our favorite television shows together. We would sit on our black l-shaped sectional couch in our living room and watch our favorite comedies. Our best-loved programs were the Big Bang Theory, Friends and How I Met Your Mother. The Big Bang Theory is about a group of four highly intellectual social misfits and their hot looking female neighbor. We watched the cult classic for many years. We would try to characterize each other and say who each one of us is like the actors in the show. My kids would emphatically say that my wife's and I relationship was eerily similar to that of Penny and Leonard in the show. I was really smart like Leonard and also practical but a little socially awkward. Penny was beautiful and practical. They had an enduring but sometimes tumultuous relationship. Maybe my kids were right. In the show Friends, they said I was like monotonic and pragmatic Ross and my wife was like Rachel. They were probably right. In How I Met Your Mother, the main character is a hapless romantic named Ted that is searching for his perfect wife. The show is about the love-struck Ted and his group of quirky friends and the antics they get into during this quest. In the show you never really meet Ted's future wife and the mother of his children. Ted is telling the story to his children about how he met their mother. My kids said I was a lot like Ted. In a way they were right. I wanted to write a book about my life before marrying my wife, settling down and having children. I wanted to explain how and why I go to where I got in life. I wanted to elaborate about the serious events that shaped and defined me. I wanted to remember the fun times and antics and tomfoolery. These stories are the result of a desire to communicate this with my children and other people.

Earlier this year at the end of January I was sitting in my basement playing the classic Eagles song Tequila Sunrise on my guitar. Jessica was sitting on the opposite loveseat working on her computer. Natalie and she had just returned from visiting Rachel earlier at Thompson Rivers University in Kamloops. It was 6 o'clock in the early evening in the middle of the winter doldrums. All of a sudden I felt like I was falling asleep. I tried to snap out of it. I felt an unusual sensation on the right side of my head and face. It was like a numbness. I went outside to get some fresh air. I went upstairs to get an aspirin. Later that week after a battery of medical tests including blood tests, ecg or electro-cardiogram and computerized axial tomography or cat scan, it was determined that I had a TIA or transient ischemic attack otherwise known as a mini-stroke. Things improved, but it was enough to scare me into realizing the frailties of life. Nothing is for certain.

As a result, after doing some soul searching, I decided to write this book. I felt I needed to write down my life experiences in a cogent manner. A gift perhaps to my children or a small legacy for posterity. In the words of Doris Day in her popular song Que sera sera, "whatever will be will be." Like everybody, I have had many life experiences, some good and some bad. I have come to the profound realization that life is short, transient and ephemeral. We should strive to make the most of the experiences that we are having here. Every day is a special gift. Finally, in the words of Henry Thoreau, "Pause avast, why so seemingly fast and deadly slow."

Uncle Mickey the Barber

36792808R00080

Made in the USA
San Bernardino, CA
02 August 2016